RAILWAY LIFE

DENNIS SCOTT

This book is dedicated to all the men and women who started the present railway system and built all the branch lines that provided the transport of goods and people across Queensland.

Copyright © 2017 Dennis Scott

All rights reserved. No part of this publication may be reproduced, stored in a retrieval system, or transmitted in any form or by any means, electronic, mechanical, photocopying, recording or otherwise, without the prior written permission from the publisher.

Every effort has been made to ensure that this book is free from error or omissions. Information provided is of general nature only and should not be considered legal or financial advice. The intent is to offer a variety of information to the reader. However, the author, publisher, editor or their agents or representatives shall not accept responsibility for any loss or inconvenience caused to a person or organisation relying on this information.

Book production services by BookCoverCafe.com

ISBN:
978-0-6480522-0-3 (pbk)
978-0-6480522-1-0 (e-bk)

Early Memories of Maryborough

I grew up in Maryborough, Queensland, about three hours' drive north of Brisbane. The population at the time was roughly twenty thousand, and as a child it seemed to me like a large town. In the fifties and sixties Maryborough had many industries, including Walkers shipyards, which built ships as well as steam engines for the railways. There were also three big sawmills, plus many cane fields in the surrounding area.

My dad, Stan Scott, was raised on a farm in a small country town called Bauple, thirty minutes' drive south of Maryborough. His parents, who were both born in Gympie, married in 1907. Dad was one of nine siblings. As an adult, my dad moved to Maryborough for work, where he met my mother, Phyllis Sager. They were married there in 1942.

My mum was born in Maryborough to a German father and English mother, who had both immigrated to Maryborough with their families.

My mother was four in 1927 when she witnessed her mother, May Sager, hit by an exploding gas cylinder, which came from the factory across the road from where the family lived. Her mother died of her injuries and the subsequent newspaper story has become part of early Maryborough history. One of my mum's brothers, Colin, was also on the veranda that day, and although both children witnessed the terrible accident, none were injured. Her other brother Ron, was was inside in his cot asleep.

My eldest brother, Robert, was born in 1942, my only sister Lorraine in 1945, and then, at two-year intervals, came my other brother Stuart and me. We were all born at Maryborough Hospital. I was the baby of the family for ten years, and that became my identity. Then my youngest brother Neil was born in 1959.

1924

persen.

Hour of horror

October 3: When Messrs. Denham's bulk store (the old Temperance Hall) in Richmond Street, caught fire yesterday, it lit a train, which led to many sensational incidents. It was a fierce blaze, which completely gutted the store and its contents. When the ammonia gas cylinders in this inferno exploded as a result of the heat, the concussion was comparable to that produced by a high explosive shell, and as these detonations continued at intervals, they suggested in imagination that the city was being bombarded by enemy guns. It was an hour of horror, during which life was endangered by the huge steel cylinder cases, which were tossed, as if out of a giant catapult, as far as 400 yards.

It is regrettable that one of these cylinders, which crashed through a house opposite the store, should have resulted in Mrs F W Sager sustaining serious injury. However, her two children, who were sleeping in the room, which was wrecked about them, escaped unscathed, despite the fact that the bed on which they were lying was crumpled up and covered with debris.

Granma Sager's death

I remember at the time feeling as though I had lost my identity and I reacted with jealousy towards Neil. Despite these feelings, I tried to ensure that I always treated my younger brother kindly and I spent as much time as possible with him. Years later we discussed this issue at length, and I was surprised at how much detail Neil could remember about my bad feelings. We talked about why I had reacted that way towards him, and these discussions benefited both of us.

Dad worked for Caltex Fuel Supply, driving a truck that delivered drums of fuel to the surrounding cane farms. My dad was a very strong man; as a child I was amazed at the ease with which he handled the empty and full forty-four-gallon drums of petrol when he loaded the truck.

During the school holidays, Dad took me with him when he went on these farm trips. I enjoyed this immensely; the truck was bright red and I sat in the front seat, which seemed high to me. This made me feel very important, and I would wave to all the other cars we passed on the road. When we arrived at a farm, Dad always talked with the farmer for a while. He was a good talker and well liked by his customers, so he was often invited inside.

Sometimes I went inside with him, but I also remember many times when I sat in the truck and waited for him to return. I must have been six years old at the time. For some reason, I always felt that something was going to happen to my dad while he was inside one of these houses. It never did, of course. Most of the time I fell asleep in the front seat on the way back to the depot.

Dad was a member of Western Suburbs Football Club and took on many roles, including team masseur and selector. When I was fifteen, my two brothers and I played junior football for the club, and our dad was always there to watch.

One time I played a really good game, and that night my dad said to me, 'You played well, why don't you play that way all the time?'

I received an award for best and fairest player for that game.

At fifteen I was six feet one inch tall (1.85 metres), and because I was very lean I looked even taller. When people met me for the first time they always asked, 'How tall are you?' This gave me a complex about my height, and when my photo was taken I always stooped to appear shorter.

I attended Central Primary School and Maryborough High School. For me, schooling was terrible. I found study hard. I could look at a schoolbook for hours and not remember a thing about what I'd just read, and this was reflected in my results. I spent a fair amount of time sitting at the back of the class, where I conspired with others to disrupt the class.

I enjoyed primary school, however, because I wasn't required to do much in lessons, and there were plenty of sporting events on hand. I loved the small bottle of milk we received every day, and on occasion I would sneak a second one.

But I hated the dancing we did every week, when the boys were paired off with the girls in the class. It wasn't that I didn't like girls; it was more a case of being picked on if I spent too much time talking to them. And of course I preferred to dance with the girls because the only other option was to dance with the boys, and this meant copping more stick.

Every week the class walked to our swimming lessons at the local pool about ten minutes from the school, and at the end of each year, at break-up time, the whole school walked to the local theatre and watched a movie. It was about a kid catching a fish. I guess the school only had access to one movie because I remember watching the same kid catch a fish three times.

I can't remember ever receiving the cane at primary school, a situation that was not to continue in high school.

In my high school years, I spent a lot of time in the headmaster's office, receiving my daily dose of the cane. I was quite a cheeky kid who often seemed to be in the wrong place at the wrong time. The cane was a piece of bamboo as big around as a little finger; bamboo was used because it had a whippy action when it came into contact with an outstretched hand. The offending pupil had to hold out their hand in front of their body with all fingers fully extended.

On one memorable day, a toilet bowl was blown up with a bundle of threepenny bungers tied together. The bungers cost three pence each, and were the biggest firecrackers available. The whole school was assembled and the culprit asked to come forward. There was no movement, so the teachers walked along the rows and selected four kids they believed were responsible. I was one of the four.

We were paraded before the whole school and encouraged to admit to our crime, but of course none of us surrendered. We were given six strokes with the cane on the top of our fingers, and we received another six underneath. It hurt—but it hurt even more knowing that I was innocent. I'm fairly positive that our French teacher (whom we nicknamed 'Frenchie') was one of the main interrogators in the dunny parade.

I felt bad about the outcome, but I never told Mum or Dad because, in the past, whenever I'd 'told tales' on the school I'd received a talking to from my dad.

One of the teachers was nicknamed 'Spitfire', and it was not because he loved planes. Anyone sitting in the front row almost needed a raincoat. I was lucky because I sat at the back of the class. Spitfire's real name was Mr Biggs, and he was actually one of the better teachers, one I could relate to.

By year nine I had become bored with schooling. I didn't enjoy the lessons and I found it hard to adjust to each teacher's different approach. Then I found a way of escaping the tedium.

The classroom was on the ground floor, and the old wooden floor had cracks between the floorboards. I discovered a manhole at the back of the room on one side, and from that day I had a way of escaping any lesson I hated. Often another boy (whose name escapes me now) would join me in my cave.

This continued for a while without incident, but I couldn't help taking it one step further. The teacher sat at his desk at the front of the class. One day I crawled under the floorboards to where I thought he was sitting above me at his desk, and I knocked on the floor. I could tell from his footsteps that each time I knocked, he walked to the door to see who was there. Each time, the class erupted with laughter.

Eventually the teacher twigged. He opened the manhole and ordered me to come out. Then he sent me to the headmaster's office.

The groundsman was instructed to secure the manhole with four screws, and this particular teacher made a point of checking it regularly. It was untouched for a while, but my partner in crime and I still needed a diversion from lessons. We brought in a screwdriver and hacksaw and filed away the bottoms of the screws, leaving only the tops visible. Soon we were back in our hidey-hole once again.

When this particular teacher, now aware of possible mischief, noticed that I was not in class he would walk to the manhole and check that the screws were in place. Our ruse worked until, becoming overconfident, we lit up our cigarettes. The smoke wafted up through the floorboards, and for the last time I was ordered to vacate the cave. This time the headmaster gave me a double dose of the cane.

I enjoyed playing football at high school, when we competed against other high schools close to Maryborough. I have a photo of the team taken in 1963. I'm in the middle row, and behind me is a person whose face later appeared on TV. Bruce Paige read the Channel

9 news for a long time and now presents the Gold Coast News. He was always a very eloquent speaker, and a nice guy to boot.

School Footy Team

I also played cricket for my schoolhouse side, Moreton. My cricket captain was Geoff Dymock, and we played a game against one of his fast-bowling rivals. The two boys enjoyed competing against each other to see who could achieve the most wickets in the season.

We were batting, had just lost two quick wickets and it was my turn to bat. Geoff's rival was on a hat trick. Geoff's advice to me was not to get out, and above all not give this particular bowler his hat trick. That was a silly thing to say, as I went LBW first ball. Luckily I didn't hear the comment Geoff made when this happened.

Another memorable sporting event was when Wesley Hall, the West Indian cricketer, came to our school in 1963. Our fast bowlers played against him, and Hall hit the balls so far our team had trouble finding them.

I tried army cadets at high school, but spent most of my time running around the oval with my arms above my head as punishment for lack of obedience. It wasn't the discipline I objected to, but the fact that I didn't appreciate someone only one year older yelling at me all the time. I recognised that I had a very real disregard for authority, which was always landing me in trouble, so I decided it would be best for me to hand in my rifle.

I was now doing a repeat of year nine because the previous year's results had been so bad. I was in a different classroom, which was manhole free. My first-term results were good and I enjoyed the feeling of being in a class with the smarter students, but during the second term I began to feel that the rest of the class was catching up to me.

Then it came time for the second-term exams. Before the chemistry exam I wrote some symbols and notes on a piece of paper, folded it and put it in my top pocket.

My cheating plan came done when Mr Biggs discovered me pulling the piece of paper from my pocket. I spent time with the headmaster once again, who sent me back to class to complete my chemistry exam.

When I walked back into the classroom I felt ashamed that I'd been caught cheating. I knew how bad it must have looked to the rest of the class. Mr Biggs put me in the front row, and that walk through the classroom seemed to last forever; I could feel every set of eyes watching me.

Ironically, I actually passed the exam with fifty-nine percent. Although none of the questions related to what I'd written on the piece of paper, however, I wasn't allowed to keep the marks I did earn. I was totally embarrassed and ashamed. I believe this incident contributed to my decision to leave school at a young age.

Growing up in Maryborough offered a good lifestyle, and there was always something interesting to see. The ships built at Walkers were launched into the Mary River. The river was not very wide and the bigger ships had to be turned as they were launched.

The steam engines, when completed, had to travel through town to the local shunting yard for dispatch. They always looked very shiny and their black paintwork glistened in the sun.

One occasion we children always looked forward to was fireworks night every November. We saved our pennies all year and then bought our stock for the big event. All the kids in the neighbourhood did the same, so it was a very colourful night.

One fireworks night the worst possible thing happened when my siblings and I lit our skyrocket. It took off and then turned into a fizzer, coming back to ground very quickly and landing in our box of crackers, which all exploded at once. Our special occasion that year lasted for about two minutes. The next year we made sure we placed the fireworks box away from the action.

The tinkling noise, that the local milkman made at four each morning, when delivering full milk bottles and removing the empties. The one chore we children loved, was collecting the milk before sunrise. This chore was made harder, after sampling the cream content that sat on the top of each bottle, and then replacing the cap.

Another most wanted chore, was collecting the fresh baked loaf of unsliced bread from the bakery, and finding new ways to take chuncks from the middle, all the time thinking this went undetected.

When it came to bathing, there was a definite order among my brothers and I. The eldest went first, and the youngest last. The procedure started with about four inches of hot water in the bath along with some cold water. For ten years I was the youngest, and by the time my turn came the water was dirty and at times had a yellow tinge to it, thanks to my brothers who went before me. Our sister Lorraine was allowed the luxury of having her own bath water.

In Maryborough, the main form of transport was pushbikes. In fact, it was known as 'the pushbike town'.

I remember being asked by interstate travellers from Victoria and New South Wales where they could see all the bikes every afternoon. This rumour was, I believe, started by travellers who returned home with descriptions of the many old colonial homes in Maryborough—and the hundreds of pushbike riders from Walkers.

At five o'clock every afternoon, the workers were allowed to ride four abreast and take up the whole road while proceeding through the town centre. Any cars travelling these streets at this time were ordered by the police to pull over to the side of the road and allow the riders free passage. Usually the number of pushbike riders lessened as the workers stopped at various hotels along the main street.

Most boys from about the age of ten years, including myself, had paper rounds. We delivered the morning paper to residents' front yards, starting daily at four in the morning. We all wore short pants, even in winter, when the temperature could drop to two or three degrees. In addition, I didn't have a pair of shoes.

We rode our pushbikes into town every morning and waited for the delivery truck to arrive from Brisbane on its way to Bundaberg. After receiving our bundle of papers, we rode to the newsagency and wrapped up each newspaper into a roll, securing it with a rubber band. We acquired these rubber bands by asking the two bike shops in town for any used tubes, which we then cut into small rubber bands.

When we had wrapped the papers, we placed them in old fruit boxes that we'd begged from the fruit shops. The handlebars on our bikes were the old type that curled up on each side and the fruit boxes fitted neatly between them.

I had a number of different ways of picking up spending money, including collecting cow manure from nearby paddocks. I vividly remember the feel of fresh manure running between my fingers. Dad bought sacks of chicken feed from the produce store, and when they were empty he stored them in the garage for our mud-crab excursions. They also happened to be perfect for my manure-collecting business. I sold each bag to our neighbours for twenty pence.

Another of my moneymaking enterprises was to sell outdated newspapers to the butcher, who used them to wrap the meat for his customers. He paid me ten pence (or one shilling) for each pound of paper.

I got my first pair of long pants and suit jacket when I was twelve years old. They were hand-me-downs and didn't fit properly; the bottoms of the pants were cut off and the waist was way too big. The first time I dressed up in my new suit and shoes was a Saturday night, when we went to the cinema. I remember feeling very special.

On weekends my siblings, with our dad, would all go to one of the creeks and collect a bag of good-sized mud crabs. We would then help our dad cook them in Mum's washing copper, and she was never happy come Monday morning to find a dirty ring around the rim. I took mud-crab sandwiches to school and swapped them for lovely jam ones.

During my early years, Maryborough had a couple of massive floods.

Crossing the Mary River, which snaked around the town on the southern side, was the Lamington Bridge, and on the northern side of the town was the Granville Bridge, which gave access to the suburb of Granville. The Lamington Bridge had detachable railings on both sides, which had to be removed as the waters started rising.

RAILWAY LIFE

The original port of Maryborough had served as a drop-off point for shiploads of overseas immigrants, and the town of Maryborough sprang up close by. The Mary River circled around the other side of the small town, and the distance between both parts of the river was only a few kilometres. During floods, the water came from both sides.

I once drove to the top of Walkers Hill and got in a rowboat to reach Dad's workplace, which was near the river. The place was flooded with three metres of water and all the empty petrol drums were floating.

Another strong memory related to the fuel depot is of the sawmill next door. When the supply boats came from Fraser Island, the bridge was raised for the boats to dock at the sawmill for unloading. I found this procedure exciting to watch, as the workers manually rotated the large wheel that opened and closed a section of the bridge to allow passage.

Maryborough had a local railway workshop, which employed about two hundred people. Once a year they provided a railway picnic using funds raised by the local staff. This was a great time for the local kids as the event was held at Torquay Beach, which was a part of Hervey Bay. Transport was provided in the form of three steam trains, which conveyed parents and kids to the railway siding at Torquay. On arrival at Torquay, a Scottish pipe band led the tribe down the hill to the beach. Parents parked on both sides of the roadway to watch their children's arrival. A tent was set up on the beachfront, and all the kids received a bag of goodies.

When I was finally allowed to travel by myself on the train, I felt like I was king of the world and had finally achieved railway-picnic status.

I loved Christmas Eve, when our family went to Queen's Park, along with most of the town. There was a raffle for the chance to win a cooked ham for Christmas, but I can't remember our family ever winning one; I only remember eating one of our chooks from our own pen every year.

One Christmas our parents told us that we would be having the rooster, and we were excited to finally be getting rid of this beast that attacked us every time we went into the pen. It looked delicious sitting on the table, but no one could eat it because it was too tough.

On Saturdays, Mum gave each of us children twenty pence (or 'two bob', as we knew it then) to go to the cinema and enjoy the movies. As time progressed, and kissing girls became an attractive way of spending my time, I worked out other ways to use the canvas theatre seats.

The midday meal on Sundays was always a roast, and then we were off to the football game. In the evening we went downtown for a Snow Cone ice cream and to watch the Salvation Army band march to their hall.

The highlight of my week was window-shopping in the main street, mainly on Friday nights. I really loved this walk, since most shops had displays in their windows. At that time no one in Maryborough had a television, unlike Brisbane, but in the early 1960s a drive-in cinema was constructed on the outskirts of town. This meant the end of the local cinemas.

Mum hated the sugar-cane season, particularly the cane-burning process, which usually happened in the afternoon when the clothesline was full of clean washing. The black ash drifted over and made its way onto the hanging clothes, which meant us children had to scamper around trying to get the clothes off the line before they were covered in soot.

Mondays and Thursdays were washing days. Before Mum could light the copper to heat the water, any mud-crab stains had to be scrubbed off. Then she placed the first load of washing in the copper. When it was finished, she pulled everything out of the boiling water with her washing stick and placed it in the wooden washing trolley.

She then transferred the washing into one of the two tubs in the laundry, which were filled with cold water and dobs of Bluo. After leaving them to soak for a while, she put everything through the manual wringer and into the second tub for a final rinse. Then she put it all through the wringer again and took it out to the clothesline.

The clothesline consisted of four lengths of wire stretching across the backyard from one wooden mast to another. The height of the wires could be adjusted using a couple of lengths of timber, which Mum raised or lowered depending on the height she wanted the line.

In the late afternoon she took the washing from the line into the kitchen, where she folded it. During this process she often sprinkled water from a bottle over everything to make the ironing easier. Irons in those days were very basic; steam irons were unknown. She usually did the ironing after the evening meal.

My involvement in the ironing process was to do all the handkerchiefs. We were all given chores, starting with washing and drying the dishes. I made extra money since my sister often paid me a few bob to do some of her chores.

Looking back, I'm amazed at the amount of work Mum accomplished every day. She was very houseproud, and tireless in carrying out her household duties. All the years I spent watching Mum go through this, week after week, must have rubbed off on me, because I'm proud to say that I adopted her house pride in my later years. But how things have changed now with all our modern automatic machines.

By the time I was fourteen and a half, life at school was suiting me less and less. I approached Mum and Dad and asked for their permission to leave school. They said that if I was able to find work, I could leave straightaway.

Within two days I had found a job on a dairy farm at Boompa, about one hour's drive from Maryborough. I recall the sense of freedom I felt when I walked out the school gate for the last time—nearly forgetting to collect my bike from the rack.

Start of My Working Life

I began work on the Fords' dairy farm at Boompa, which was near Biggenden. On my first day I was given a horse and dog to use, which made me feel great because I'd always loved animals. Every morning at four I saddled my horse and rounded up the cows for milking, which I did seven days a week. During the time between morning and evening milking, I did chores around the farm.

I was working eighty hours per week for a monthly wage of ten pounds. When it was time for my three days off, I travelled home to Maryborough, where I bought my supply of cigarettes and visited friends and neighbours.

I travelled home by rail motor, known as 'red hares' because of their bright red colour. Used as people movers in those days, they had a prominent radiator at the front beneath the one large window. The driver sat in the front on the right, where he could operate the clutch and gears.

Red Hare Rail Motor

While at the Boompa farm, I started my own garden and also built a chicken coop for all the chicks that hatched. An important role for me was to milk the cows twice a day.

I processed the milk using a manually operated separator, by means of a rotating handle and a spinning separator. The milk made its way through the system, coming out as cream and milk through different exits. An important part of this role was to soak the individual pieces of the separator in boiling water and dry them before operation. The cream was sent away to the butter factory, and the remaining milk was fed to the newborn calves.

I enjoyed this work; in fact, I enjoyed all the work involved with the dairy. The only time I hated the milking was when the magneto on the engine operating the milking machines broke, which usually meant a delay of three days before we got a new one. While we waited, the owner and I had to do the milking by hand, and the process took twice as long. This happened three times and I remember them all very clearly.

After milking, I spent my time fixing gates and fences until lunch at midday. After lunch, I had two-hour break, which I usually spent working in the garden or sneaking a cigarette in my room. I had my own room in the barn, where I enjoyed listening to my small transistor radio. I once heard a noise coming from above my room and, on investigation, found a huge carpet snake asleep. After this discovery, I closed my window every night.

On Sundays, after milking, I was allowed to take the horse and go fishing in a nearby creek. I often came home with some lovely freshwater fish, which I skinned for our dinner.

I performed my milking duties with the owner's son, Fred, and I also enjoyed the company of Molly Ford, the owner's wife. She made me feel welcome, and we often talked while we did the dishes each night. It was a great way to keep my mind off missing my family and home.

On Christmas Day 1963, I went out on the horse to round up the cows for milking. The horse was cantering when it made a sudden stop at the local waterhole for a drink and I slid into the water—an unexpected Christmas-day swim!

I loved the work and lifestyle on the farm. Not only was it enjoyable, but I also achieved the self-discipline and work ethic school had not provided. I achieved this with the support and love the Ford family gave me, and I've always been grateful to them for giving me a great start to my working life. But even at this young age I knew I couldn't make the farm my career, so after eleven months I left and returned to Maryborough.

While I'd been away on the farm, there had been some changes at home. Neil was now the only sibling still living at home, Robert was working away in the railway,

Lorraine was working at the hospital in Kingaroy, and Stuart had moved to Perth.

After returning to Maryborough, I worked for a while for the owner of the corner shop, Mr Ray. As a young child, in order to get money I used to steal his empty soft-drink bottles and cash them in for the deposit, but my purpose now was different. My work this time was manual, and consisted of digging holes for the foundation of new rooms Mr Ray was building to accommodate his family.

I applied for a position with Queensland Railway as a lad porter. A lad porter's duties consisted of sweeping the platforms, cleaning the carriages, collecting tickets on the passenger trains, unloading parcels from mail carriages, looking after the cloakroom and cleaning the windows on the rail motors.

While I waited to hear back from the railway, I worked at the abattoir on the chicken assembly line. It was horrible work and I couldn't wait for my time there to finish.

As youngsters, my friends and I would lie about our age. When I was nearly sixteen, Bob Potter, Gary Sheehy and I started buying beer every Friday night. This was usually a large bottle of Pilsener, and after consuming it we would ride our pushbikes into town and act like idiots.

When we were nearly seventeen, we found a local hotel that served us beers from ten to eleven most Saturday mornings.

I thought no one knew about it, but years later Dad told me that the police had known all along.

My eldest brother Robert brought home a lot of stories from his work on the railway. One such story was when he was locked away in the coffin chamber on the mail train, and went for a ride for two stations before being released. The coffin chamber was situated up high at the end of some vans that worked the mail trains. When the chambers were in use, liquid was placed on the chamber floor. Although the chamber was empty on this particular day, there was still some liquid there, and after his unfortunate trip of twenty-five minutes Robert emerged with most of his clothing saturated with the smelly fluid. After a change of clothing, he went back to work for the rest of his shift. This story stuck in my memory and came back to haunt me later when I was a lad porter.

I Started work for the railways in June 1965. I dressed for my first day in long black serge pants, a black vest with silver buttons, and a hat with the front brim tilted down and worn on the side of my head. I felt a million dollars.

My first day was exciting, and I was anxious to do whatever I was told. The chief stationmaster, Mr Eagers, was fully dressed in his railway uniform, complete with white pith helmet. With his thumbs hooked into his garters, he stood above me as I polished the section of rail that had assigned to me by the platform foreman to maintain. He asked my name, remarked that it must be my first day, told me I was doing a sterling job, and encouraged me to keep up the great work.

The second week was known as 'initiation week'. This was not a formal introduction to the railways as much as a not-so-friendly orientation. I was subjected to three or four lots of sawdust, grease and oil mixed together and plastered around my genitals. My mother quickly got sick of doing the washing, so things soon stopped.

First pay docket

Maryborough Station was a dead-end station, and mail trains that arrived had to be pulled out by another engine. All other trains went around the angle at Baddow Station and continued to Gympie or Bundaberg.

Since not all mail trains came into Maryborough Station, part of our job as lad porters was to travel out to Baddow by engine and van, and return with passengers and luggage.

Another of our jobs was sweeping out the assistant's office every shift. We followed the same procedure every time: we placed sawdust and kerosene mixture on the floor and then cleaned it all up. This technique was meant to stop excess dust from forming on all the paperwork in the office.

One story I heard involved a group of lad porters who were sent to Baddow to retrieve a dog from the dog box. The dog box was positioned at about shoulder height at the rear of the guard's van at the back of the train. When the boys opened the door, the dog jumped over their shoulders and ran for the bushes. As time was limited, they quickly replaced the dog with a local station cattle dog, and it was duly sent north.

I quickly decided on a good work ethic for myself; I would take after my mother with regard to cleaning, and I would emulate my father's communication skills.

Dad was a good talker, and I'd noticed how well he got along with his customers with this method. I set these goals in place.

Ken Scott and I met and became friends when we both played junior football. Ken had started work twelve months previously with the railways. He was the eldest of four children; he had two brothers and one sister. Ken's father, George, worked at the local sawmill and coached us in junior rugby league, and his mother, Edna, was a stay-at home mum.

Ken met his girlfriend, Rae Scougall, during the Easter holidays in 1963 at Hervey Bay, when Rae was working but Ken was still attending high school. My first pay, in pre-decimal days, was nineteen pounds for the fortnight. On paydays we all paid our bills at the local cigarette shop and then went to the Mimosa Cafe for lunch. This was where Rae worked, so we were starting a good friendship.

Rae's father, Charlie, worked as a carpenter in the local railway workshops, and her mother, Eunice, devoted her time to raising her six children. Despite the tough circumstances, there was always food on the table for the family and extras for visitors.

On the first occasion Rae took Ken home to meet her parents, her father Charlie asked Ken if he had a job, a dog and a bank account, and if his father had a car. Ken's answers must have impressed Charlie, because he pulled a jellybaby from his pocket, bit off the head and handed the rest to Ken. That was how you could tell in those days if someone was considered a suitable boyfriend for a daughter.

Rae's father Charlie liked to frequent the local Lamington Hotel as often as he could, and some Saturday evenings he also arrived home with a friend for a meal. After eating, he would get the children to sing their favourite song, 'I'm a Little Teapot.' They all performed their individual roles, and even after all these years, after a little lubrication they still break into that same song.

On Sunday mornings, Charlie took his children to the dump, where they scrounged what they could in the form of batteries, radiators, tyres and sump oil. Charlie placed in the batteries a couple of Bex powders and was able to get enough charge for the week. He put pepper into the radiators, which sealed any leaks for a while. Any tyre that had any tread at all was also useful to Charlie, and he kept his motor topped with the sump oil. He was a very resourceful man.

Rae's mother was also very inventive. When the Olympic Games were held in Melbourne in 1956, she bought some material depicting the games and made dresses for each of the girls.

In 1957, on one of the family's trips home from the bay, all the children and the dog were in the back seat of the car they called 'the terror plane', which had a hole in the floor the air breezed through. To plug it up, they rolled some clothing into a bundle and shoved it into the hole. As they were approaching Half Way Hill, smoke appeared inside the car. The bundle of clothing had made its way onto the exhaust pipe and started a fire.

As luck would have it, someone following behind them had just purchased a fire extinguisher and was happy to jump out and put it to use. The fire was extinguished, but in that bundle of clothing was Rae's new dress made of her favourite Olympic material.

Some of my duties as a lad porter involved relieving at places like Baddow and Pialba. At Baddow one of the jobs was to collect all the kerosene lamps from the signal poles that lit the signals for the oncoming drivers. There were about thirty or so signals, and we used a push-pull trike that ran on the track with one dolly wheel on one rail and two wheels on the other rail. We hung two broom handles on the back of the trike to hold the lamps we collected.

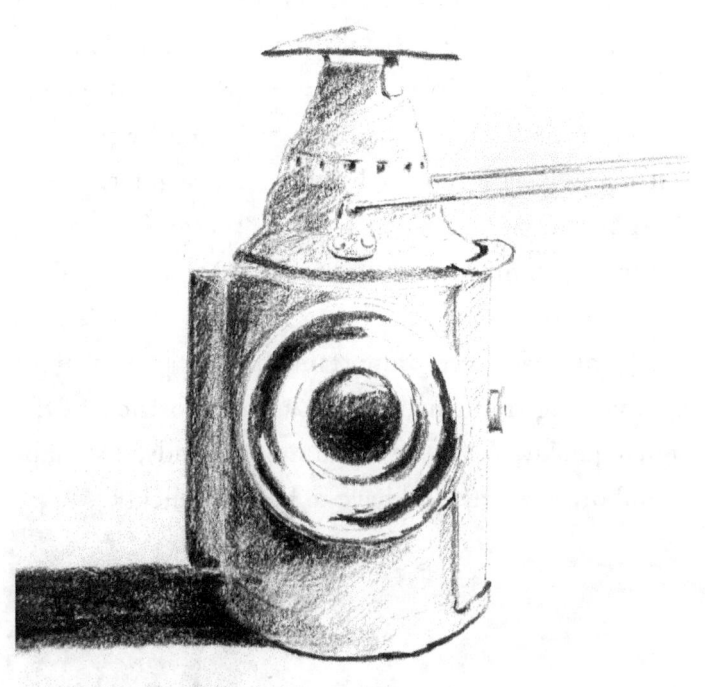

Kerosene signal lamp

The operator sat on the side that had the two wheels on the track, with his feet operating the bottom pedals and his arms operating the top half. It was easy to reach great speed with the push-and-pull action, but often when we went too fast around a bend the smaller dolly wheel would lift and derail the trike.

On one occasion when returning from the Gympie end on a downhill run, I noticed the station officer looking out the cabin window. When I was under the set of points he pulled the lever, and the lamps, trike and I went three different ways. I was the only person not laughing.

The lamps had to be refilled, the glass cleaned, the wicks trimmed and the whole thing inspected by the stationmaster before being returned to the signal pole. This was a very important role, because at night approaching trains had to pick up the position of the signal quickly. When it was raining or windy, the lamps would often go out and have to be relit quickly.

One person rail trike

Another job I was assigned, along with other lad porters, was the cleaning of the windows on the 'red hares'. The rail motors were stabled in a shed on one side of the yard. Often, after cleaning the windows, we would sit in the driver's seat in the first carriage with the passengers playing with the gears and throttle. One day we started up the rail motor, drove out to the signal and then reversed to the stop blocks. It was great fun.

Later, a new silver rail motor arrived to replace the rail motors. This was a little different from what we were used to so we never attempted to drive it, but we did try out the fire extinguisher and found that the foam from one of them just about filled up the cabin. What a mess to clean up!

On certain runs to Howard and Pialba, lad porters, acting as guards, worked the rail motors. On certain occasions I was assigned this job and it made me feel special. I especially liked the run to Howard, as there were nice-looking girls to watch out for.

During my stint at Maryborough, I came into contact with train drovers who travelled with the stock to Brisbane, sometimes being away from home for two weeks or more. As well as their swags, they carried battery jiggers to help get the animals back on their feet. The drovers, who normally had a compartment in the guard's van, checked the stock when trains went into the sidings.

During my time with the drovers, I was still quite cheeky and I always bantered with them. One day a train drover was walking along the platform in front of me, and I rushed past and knocked his hat off. He was carrying a glass of water, which he threw onto my pants, so I turned and gave him more cheek, saying that water wouldn't hurt me. The next thing I knew, he aimed his jigger at the wet spot, turned it up high and pushed the button. Holy cow! I now knew why the cattle always let out anguished cries. From that moment on this particular drover became my best friend.

My worst fear came was realised one night when the foreman said I was to retrieve a coffin from the incoming mail train. With the help of the funeral director and another porter, I pushed the barrow up to the carriage, hopped up and unlocked the door. The first thing I noticed was the liquid that my brother had told me about.

I pulled the coffin out of the chamber and, with the help of the others, put it on the barrow. It seemed too easy, but then the porter told me that I now had to make sure I placed the belts back in the chamber properly, which meant getting back up on the barrow and closing the door. I did it very quickly, as bad thoughts came to me, and slammed the door shut.

I was fortunate enough to ride in the cab of a Bayer Garrett steam engine. These were huge red shining engines with the water tank at the front. These engines were good load pullers, and they were used on stock trains for this purpose, but the water tanks derailed easily.

Although I was enjoying my time as a lad porter, I felt the need to get out of the country environment. Thinking that Brisbane could offer a more promising career, I left the railway in 1966 and made the move south.

Biscuits, Boots and Boarding Houses

I arrived in Brisbane in late 1966 and met up with my mate, Bob Potter. We leased a small flat in Paddington together and I secured a job at Arnott's biscuit factory, where Bob also worked. The flat was close to the city and work, and not far from the shops. It consisted of a bedroom and a separate kitchen, and the use of a communal bathroom. Bob and I stayed there for about four months.

I found production-line work very different to railway life. I wasn't sure whether I liked it, but I decided to give it my best shot. My job was boring and tedious; I did the same thing all day long. Later, I was assigned several other tasks, and I must have impressed someone because after two months I found myself being taught how to be a baker in charge of a biscuit machine. This I really enjoyed, but as time went on I realised that working at Arnott's was not what I wanted for my long-term career. I lasted at Arnott's for about four months.

I secured another job at a boot factory across the road from the old Lang Park football ground. The pay was a little better than the biscuit factory, and I began to enjoy learning the trade of making shoes, but I was now thinking often about my previous work in Maryborough. I decided that the railway was where my future lay. After five months I left the boot factory destined for a career on the railways.

One day, to my surprise, I ran into Rae Scougall, Ken's girlfriend from Maryborough. She explained that she and Ken had had a falling out and she had moved to Brisbane to get some clear space. We met up at least once a week and had a drink or two. At these get-togethers she talked often about Ken, and when I went home to Maryborough for weekends and met up with Ken, he talked often about Rae. Eventually I asked Rae if she wanted to get back together with Ken, and on one of my trips home I asked Ken the same question. With the help of my matchmaking skills, my two friends became a couple again and Rae moved back to Maryborough. Ken had turned eighteen by this time and was now eligible to become an acting shunter.

Life in Brisbane for a boy from the bush was exciting, especially at some of the great parties I went to, even though the minimum drinking age was twenty-one. Life in the flat came to a close when Bob decided to move in with his grandparents and I was left to find a new place of residence. I moved into a room above a fish-and-chip shop on Given Terrace in Paddington. From the kitchen window I could see the XXXX sign flashing above the brewery.

I stayed there for about three months, and then moved into a boarding house on Wickham Terrace, which just happened to be where all the railway shunters from Roma Street yard resided. During the next month I received a call from the railways, offering me a job as a lad porter at Mayne Junction Station. It was September 1967 when I resumed my railway career.

Conditions for shunters at Roma Street were precarious to say the least. There was no such thing as health-and-safety regulations in the sixties and early seventies, and, not surprisingly, there were a few accidents.

One day, when I was sitting on the front veranda of the boarding house, a man approached. He introduced himself as Paul and said he had just arrived by train from New South Wales. He asked if this was a boarding house, and where he could find the employment office for the railways. Within an hour he was back. He had secured a room in the boarding house, and was starting work in the Roma Street shunting yard at two o'clock that same day.

When Paul arrived home after his first shift, already he had stories to tell me. His first day had been quite eventful. In order to direct the shunt, he had to remember numerous signs, many of which used various parts of the body. There were twenty-six signs in total—a lot to remember in one day—and I had a great laugh as he explained each one to me.

The Roma Street yard sloped from north to south. At the northern end, the foreman would set a wagon heading south and then direct its movement—which roads that particular wagon should take—using certain hand movements to the shunter at the southern end.

Being a shunter was a dangerous occupation, and injuries often occurred. After the wagon was correctly directed, the shunter had to run alongside the wagon and apply the handbrake before the wagon hit the blocks. Sometimes he didn't manage to accomplish this and the wagon and blocks crashed together. This was very dangerous; sometimes the shunter slipped and his feet came in contact with the wheels of the wagon.

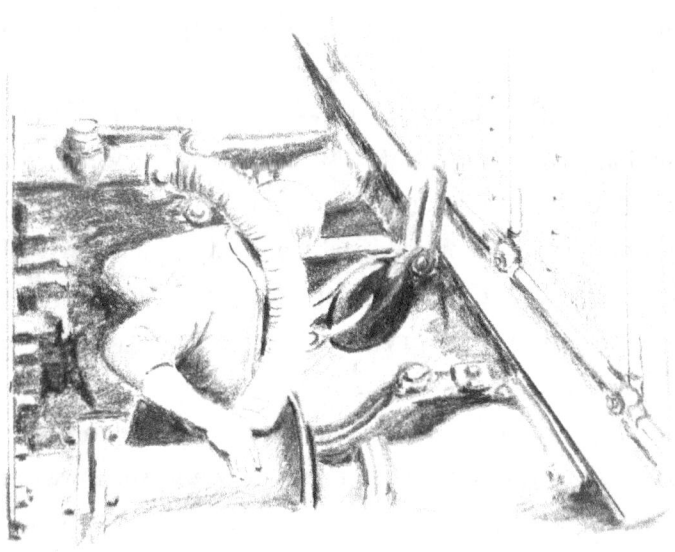

Early method of wagon attach

The couplings between wagons were of the transition type, with a swinging ball that screwed up on a thread. When attaching one approaching wagon to another, the shunter walked alongside the approaching wagon and, when the two wagons came into contact, lifted the coupling up to the hook on the other wagon. The couplings were very heavy and it required great practice to perfect the swing to complete the attach.

These types of couplings were eventually phased out and replaced with auto couplers. In the late seventies, health-and-safety regulations were tightened up and new protocols introduced. Subsequently, all prospective shunters were put through a training course before working in a shunting yard.

Roma Street, as well as being a massive shunting yard, also housed a goods complex that supplied equipment throughout Queensland. Trucks lined up every day, sometimes stretching out to the road, waiting for entry into the complex. Most of the time they were waiting for a checker to become available. The checker's job was to sit in the wagon and count as the goods were loaded into various wagons. It seemed to me that the checker's main job was just to sit on a stool.

The goods yard was full of characters. One such person I heard about was nicknamed 'Havachat'.

Havachat would walk around the complex carrying a brown envelope under his arm. When approached by a supervisor, he would say he was delivering the envelope and continued on his rounds.

In 1967, when I started work as a lad porter at Mayne, steam trains still operated in the suburban area, although they were phased out in 1969. It was a big yard, with marshalling and stabling yards for the suburban trains, and had a staff of cleaners to attend to all the suburban carriages.

All members of the staff at Mayne were friendly and I took an instant liking to my new working environment. The first assistant I worked with was Kevin Shaw, and I enjoyed his method of working with laughter.

Out front, near the office, was a massive coal chute. Each day, the shunt pushed wagons up to the top and dumped the coal for the steam engines. There were also some steam engines still working the suburban lines.

Mayne was a junction for the Ferny Grove line, and as lad porters we had to watch out for connecting passenger trains to and from that line. We also had to make sure all the doors on the old wooden carriages were closed to ensure safe passage through the tunnels to Roma Street. On Sundays we sold tickets on the rail motors on the Ferny Grove line.

It was a well-paid job. The staff at Mayne taught me all the bookwork connected with ticket selling and doing the monthly returns.

Part of our duties involved working a rail motor to Toogoolawah, and sometimes the old 'red hare' was used. On these occasions some tourists travelled just to enjoy the ride. This was a part of my duties I really enjoyed because I got to meet the girls who were travelling to schools in Ipswich. We stayed the night in quarters at Toogoolawah and returned to Brisbane in the morning.

While at Mayne, I was intrigued by the large amount of money that arrived on payday and was taken to the paymaster's office. The money arrived by taxi, with a police officer and a clerk from the paymaster's office on board. Waiting for them outside the station was a labourer with a wheelbarrow, and after the money was loaded into the wheelbarrow it was walked about six hundred metres to the pay office. It was amazingly simple and effective, but I can't imagine anyone daring to do that today.

I also liked the task of taking notices to the signal cabin. To me, the cabin seemed huge. There was a long row of small handles positioned about stomach height for the signalmen to operate the signal and points in that yard. These levers were powered by gas to make the operation easier.

On Monday, we began work at one-thirty am. Our job was to work the rail motor to Toogoolawah and then return. First we had to collect our tickets and date press from the cabin. The same signalman, Des Dodds, was always on duty. He had a stump in place of his right leg and made a loud clomping sound as he walked across the wood floor. On arrival in winter, he always offered me a small glass of rum to warm me up.

Across the road from the old Mayne signal cabin, a night officer lived with his family in a railway house. During the Brisbane Exhibition in August, his children charged cars to park on the empty railway land while they went to the 'ekka' (local parlance meaning 'exhibition'). This man was known as 'Officer D' because his last name was Dibble (Officer Dibble was a character in the cartoon series *Top Cat*), and he was a real character—one of the many I would meet in the old-style railways.

I received a call from Rae and Ken, who said they were going to be married in May the following year, 1968, and they wanted me to be best man. At this stage Ken was working in Maryborough as an acting shunter, but he was applying for shunters' positions. In November

1968 he was appointed as a shunter in Warwick, a town southwest of Brisbane.

In 1968 I was still living at the boarding house on Wickham Terrace. That year I was joined firstly by my big brother Robert, and then later by my other brother Stuart.

I travelled to Warwick to visit Rae and Ken after their son Jody was born. It was in the middle of winter, but Rae and Ken didn't have any proper heating so I purchased a bar heater for them. They told me that they'd learned the lesson that in Warwick in winter a frozen radiator was the general rule, and the trick was to empty it early in the night and refill it in the morning.

Rae told me the story of one of Ken's workmates, who worked as a kangaroo shooter on weekends. Ken had told his mate that he and Rae had a dog, so one day the guy arrived on the doorstep wearing blood-splattered clothes and handed her a kangaroo leg. 'Here, missus,' he said, 'this is for your dog.'

While in Warwick, I went with Ken to football training. The boys got into a circle and, with the cold wind blowing in their faces, passed the football around for about five minutes before heading for their cars. Ken told me they were going to continue training indoors, which I considered a good idea. When we arrived at the local pub, I considered it a *great* idea because inside the main bar was a blazing woodstove. It was the perfect way to finish off footy training.

Ken received a transfer to Maryborough as a shunter in 1970, and just after that he was accepted to attend guard-training school in Brisbane. Ken completed his training successfully and in 1971 was appointed as a guard at Emerald, a small town inland from Rockhampton.

In thinking about my own future, I considered becoming a porter, or possibly moving on to another position like shunter and number taker in the shunting yards. In the end I decided to stay away from the shunting yard, and I was encouraged to study for the night-officer exam. It was necessary to answer questions from 'the book of rules', a volume that contained all the rules pertaining to running trains and managing stations.

Remembering my experience at high school, I knew I needed to write out the entire contents of this book and memorise it. Over a period of three months, I did exactly that. I copied that book twice and then sat for the exam while it was fresh in my mind.

On my first attempt I got five questions wrong, which meant I had to resit the exam. On my second attempt, I passed. I had become an acting night officer. Now I felt really proud.

In the middle of 1970 I was appointed night officer, Toowoomba relief, and was proud to get into that grade. The night-officer grade meant I worked at staff stations. At that time, if I'd wanted to be promoted to the stationmaster grade I would've had to sit the Morse code exam. The Morse code system was dropped shortly after, however, so I was able to apply for positions higher than night officer without needing to learn Morse code.

The Girl on the Platform

My first job on the Toowoomba relief staff was to learn all the staff stations on the track between Murphys Creek, at the foot of the Great Dividing Range, and Toowoomba. It was winter, and on my first day when I tried to start my car, which was parked outside the boarding house, I couldn't get it going.

One of the other boarders who came to my assistance said it was obvious I wasn't a local. They all knew, he said, that if you parked your car outside in winter you had to put hessian bags over the radiator at night to stop it from freezing. A lesson learnt. I had to pour boiling water over the radiator to get enough water running through it to start the car and get me to the job.

Some months before I got the job at Toowoomba I had met a girl on the platform of Mayne Station. Her name was Jacqueline Nipperess, and I was immediately drawn to her because of her friendly nature and country manner. The other striking feature about her was her beautiful red hair. Jackie was brought up in Gympie and had recently moved to Brisbane to live with her sister.

We went on a few dates, but then went our separate ways. At the time I was busy writing out the book of rules in preparation for my application for the night officer's position.

Jackie was born in Gympie in December 1952. Her father was John Nipperess and her mother was Dorothy Jean Baxter. Her family consisted of elder sister Salina, younger sister Noeleen, and younger brother John.

Her mother's family had emigrated from England. Jackie's paternal great-grandfather, William Nipperess, was sent on a transport from England to Sydney Cove on 7 October 1829 for stealing a sheep from a neighbour's farm. He was convicted on 16 March 1829, and his pregnant wife Martha died five days later. The couple had three other children. He arrived at Sydney Cove on 19 February with 198 other prisoners after a 135-day journey. On arrival at Sydney Cove, he was sent to a produce farm at Baulkham Hills, just outside Sydney, which grew all the produce for the new colony.

After a period of seven years, transported convicts were allowed to apply for permission to marry. In Parramatta in 1841, William married Bridget Hall, who had come out from Ireland. William was granted a pardon in 1845, and the couple moved to Howlong, a town on the border of New South Wales and Victoria. In 1860 William was granted a public licence to operate the hotel at Howlong, and there is still a hotel operating on this site.

William and Bridget had five children, the start of that Nipperess generation in Australia. Bridget died in 1869 at the age of fifty-six, and William died in 1882 at the age of eighty-two.

Time passed after Jackie's and my few dates. One day, when I was writing out my second copy of the rule book, I found myself thinking about her and wondering what had become of her in Brisbane. I wrote her a letter and suggested we get together for drinks. She replied and we arranged to meet on a Friday night at a hotel in Brisbane.

Jackie chose the hotel, saying there was a band playing there that she wanted to see. Over a few drinks she told me that she was dating one of the band members, whose name was also Denis. I was a little deflated and felt that I might have been intruding on her night, but happily for me she soon stopped seeing the other Denis and we began to date regularly. Years later Jackie bumped into the Denis from the band, and she and I travelled to Bangkok to attend his wedding to Ann. We've all kept in touch since the wedding, and the two families have spent time together.

I passed my exam successfully and gained a position on the Toowoomba relief staff. The staff jobs on the range were mundane: crossing a few trains, operating a small signal cabin, and exchanging staff instruments, or tokens, with the crews. After a week of instruction I was given my first shift at Spring Bluff Station. This was a beautiful little station, with three railway houses for the staff and many gardens the staff took care of. Spring Bluff was very popular during Toowoomba's Carnival of Flowers in September.

Winter in Spring Bluff was very cold, but fortunately there was a wooden stove in the office. I discovered where the woodpile was, but there was no cut wood available so I looked around for an axe to chop some more but couldn't find one. When my relief staff member arrived at midnight, I explained why there was no fire. He told me they hid the axe because a certain person was in the habit of using the cut wood without ever restocking it. He showed me where the axe was, and also an emergency supply of cut wood hidden in one of the garbage bins. From then on I always made sure there was enough cut wood for the fire.

Two days later, I had to do my first detach. As I explained earlier, there was no training provided for shunting, or handling points and levers, so I was flying by the seat of my pants. I had to detach a camp wagon into a siding. I managed to detach it easily enough, but when I put my weight on the lever controlling the points to bring the diesel out of the siding, the weight went onto the ball instead of the handle, causing the road to be set incorrectly and derailing the diesel. Another lesson learned the hard way.

When it came to obtaining a staff instrument, the electric staff instruments officer had to hold down a button to allow access to the instrument. I found this operation difficult at first. I used too much vigour in trying to pull out the staff, and in those first few weeks I lost a lot of skin. It was eventually explained to me that I had to roll the staff out of the machine slowly.

I heard stories about a certain few opportunists who were desperate for a little extra cash. On receiving the staff off the last train on a Saturday night, they would bury it in the bush and report that the staff, when thrown off by the fireman, had become tangled in the undercarriage of the diesel. This meant that the staff instrument had become unbalanced and an electrician had to be called out from Toowoomba to rebalance it. This gave the men an extra four hours' pay while they waited for the electrician to arrive.

I also relieved at Holmes, Murphys Creek and Ballard Stations. The staff at Ballard had been stationed there for a long time, and because they didn't have a lot to do they'd taken to feeding an ever-increasing number of animals that turned up during the day. On my first relieving shift, I was presented with a roster of animals that would be arriving during the day and needed to be fed. So that was how I spent most of my day at Ballard Station. I resolved never to end up like those fellows.

The relief position at Holmes was very similar to the one at Spring Bluff, in that there was a small signal cabin and most of the staff had been there a long time. Like Spring Bluff, the cabin was fitted with a small potbelly stove, which made the winter nights more enjoyable.

They also had a supply of coal outside the office, so cutting firewood was not an issue.

The downhill track to Brisbane from Holmes had been set up with a runaway line, which led to a siding that went uphill—a safety feature which allowed trains with faulty braking systems to divert into the siding and come to a halt. When a train arrived at Holmes, the driver tested his brakes and then gave the all-clear signal by blowing his whistle. The train then continued on the downhill track to Brisbane.

While I was still learning the job I was told that I could block any train except one. This very important train ran from Stanthorpe, a town south of Toowoomba on the Granite Belt near the border with New South Wales that had an ideal climate for growing essential produce. The train was known as 'the fruit train'. It ran from Monday to Friday, and if on time it came through the range area just after midnight. It went straight through to the markets at Moolabin in Brisbane, which supplied most of Queensland and the east coast with fruit and vegetables.

When this train was due, I always made sure that all signals were in their proper place; even a one-minute delay at the signals meant writing a please-explain memo to the general manager.

During this early period I was finding it hard to exist on my learning wage. I was paying board and driving to Brisbane to see Jackie on my weekends off, so money was scarce. To obtain extra cash, I would hock my record player for five dollars and then buy it back on paydays. This merry-go-round continued for quite some time until my finances became more settled.

Time to Go West, Young Man

After three months of working on the range I was advised by the leave officer that I would be going to a place called Mungallala for a couple of weeks of relief duties. I didn't even know where the town was. I arrived by train at two in the morning and slept the rest of the night in the cream shed.

Mungallala was a crew-change depot situated between Roma and Charleville. It had a post office, cafe, hotel, garage and shop, plus about sixty houses. The railway station was two kilometres out of town, where there were also four railway houses for staff.

The two weeks turned into months, but I did manage to travel to Brisbane twice. I obtained accommodation at the local hotel. The people at the hotel were very hospitable, and the publican's wife provided my meals. Because of the isolation of the place, I read a lot of books during my time there. The station staff treated me well and made sure I was looked after.

The stationmaster, Jack, was on duty with me one day when a goods train stopped at the station. An argument developed between Jack and the train guard, ending with the stationmaster flat on his back on the ground. He got up, shook himself off and said, 'Every dog has its day.'

About three weeks later Jack came into the office and picked up an old axe handle from the floor. He said he was going down to meet the goods train in the yard. I thought nothing more of it—until the guard from the train came limping into the office with blood coming from a cut on his forehead. I soon worked out that every dog did indeed have his day. Not another word was spoken about the matter by either party.

Some nights I had to walk the two kilometres to the railway station in complete darkness, and the only way

I could work out where to walk was by sticking closely to the edge of the road. During my shift one night I thought I heard a cry for help, but when I went outside I couldn't see or hear anything.

At about five in the morning I heard the same cry again and I went outside. In the emerging daylight, I saw a figure slumped across the cattle grid at the main gate. When I got closer I could make out the shape of a man with his feet stuck in the grid. It was one of the Charleville crew who had been at the local pub. When walking back after midnight, he had slipped down between the rails of the cattle grid and couldn't free himself. When I asked if he was in pain, he said he couldn't feel anything because he was freezing from the winter cold.

I was still working at Mungallala just before Christmas in 1970 when the relief officer rang to say I was required to do a week's relief work at Amby, which was closer to Roma. The stationmaster at Amby, Barry Tait, said he was going to Brisbane to mow his grass. It sounded funny, but I knew he was going to spend Christmas with his family.

On my arrival at Amby I booked into the local hotel. The hotelkeeper told me that on Christmas day he and his wife were going away for the day and I would be the only person in the hotel. Before they left, he gave me half a dozen cold beers and a plate full of chicken, ham and prawns. I will never forget that Christmas Day of 1970, the only one I have ever spent alone, with no human, animal, TV or radio to keep me company.

At the seven-month mark, I rang the leave clerk and said jokingly that the women who had looked terrible when I'd first arrived in Mungallala were starting to look good now. It had the desired effect, because I was out of there the next week, transferred back to Toowoomba.

During these years, the small stations and road crossings in Queensland were staffed mainly by female stationmasters ('stationmistresses') and gatekeepers. A lot of these women had been widowed during the war and were employed by the railway all over the state. They were also supplied with railway housing. This kept most of the small country towns active as most of these places had station staff and also a number of staff who worked as fettlers. This had a flow-on effect in other areas like schools, banks, post offices and hotels. These arrangements stayed in place until the late 1970s, after which railway staff gradually moved away as stations closed.

After a small stint working in the Toowoomba area, I was sent to Inglewood to relieve. Inglewood was a crew-change station between Toowoomba and Goondiwindi, and was used for remarshalling the wheat trains before their trip up the ranges to Warwick. It was a fairly big yard with one stationmaster and two assistants. It was also a branch line for Texas, which was south of Inglewood near the border and about one and half hours' travel by train.

Most of the trains had to have a certain number of auto couplers at the front; this enabled the engine to successfully pull the fully loaded train up the range into Warwick. The rest of the train was then connected by a combination of ball-and-screw and auto couplers.

The remarshalling required quite a lot of shunting, which was performed by the guard and assistant on duty. In those days very few people were qualified in shunting. You learned how to shunt through experience on the job.

One day I was shunting one of the Warwick-bound trains into a road that had a curve in it. As it was a fairly long shunt, the guard was positioned up near the engine and I was way down the back, shunting one screw coupler onto another around this curve. I gave the signal with my kerosene lamp for the shunt to proceed on a slow green towards me. When I could see the speed of the shunt slowing down, I went in to attach the wagons.

The type of wagon I was attaching had a buffer that went back into a housing, which in turn met up with a spring to take up any slack. As I bent over the buffer to attach the coupler, it started to move back into the housing, trapping the front of my trousers. I was caught with the shunt still slowly moving backwards. I couldn't give the guard the signal to stop because he was unable to see me. My only option was to pull myself up out of my trousers. I walked out to where the guard could see me in my undies, and he couldn't stop laughing.

On another occasion we were unloading the goods from the mail train into a wagon bound for the Texas branch, and the guard was the same one who had witnessed my striptease. We came across a couple of kegs of wine, and straightaway I saw the driver and the guard exchange looks. I didn't have to be a clairvoyant to read their minds.

The goods were unloaded into the wagon and the train departed on time for Texas, but it was a bit late arriving there. It was also late arriving back into Inglewood, but no questions were asked. Apparently, on inspection at Texas it was found that one of the kegs must have sprung a very bad leak in transit.

Also at Inglewood, they had a tractor placer to shunt wagons when no engine was available. A tractor placer was a road–rail machine with a set of small pony wheels on the front that sat on the rails, with the back and front wheels riding on top of the rails.

One Friday night we had a train due in from Warwick. When I looked out at the home signal I could see it wasn't lit, so I hopped onto the tractor placer to relight the signal. As I passed through the crossing gates, I closed each one behind me. On my return, I stopped at the gates to open them. I had one half open when I heard a noise behind me. I turned around to see that the tractor placer had crept down and was in the process of running me over. I had forgotten to pull on the handbrake.

I clearly remember the thoughts that raced through my head at the time. I was terrified and had no idea what was going to be the end result. I was being dragged along under the rubber wheel, which sat on top of the rail. The tractor placer stopped when it eventually came in contact with the half-opened gate, but I was trapped underneath.

I tried to work out what damage had been done to my legs and stomach. I realised that the feeling in my left leg was different to my right. I had never been in this situation before and I was making decisions out of fear.

At the bottom end of the yard was a refreshment room where the locals used to have a few drinks. Outside the doors were the crossing gates that allowed traffic through when no trains were running. I called out for help because I knew the refreshment room was close by.

After a while the publican, who must have weighed well over one a hundred and twenty kilograms, came out. Seeing me trapped, he immediately jumped onto the tractor placer that was sitting on top of me. I felt his full weight come down, but luckily he knew how to drive the placer off me.

The publican checked me carefully, asking whether I had feeling in my legs. He wanted to remove one of my shoes to look at my left leg, but I urged him to ring for an ambulance straightaway and leave my shoe in place. While we waited he gave me a full glass of port to drink. My legs didn't feel or look good.

On arrival at hospital, the duty staff very slowly removed my pants and the shoe from my left foot. I feared the worst as I waited for the outcome. I was extremely lucky. Although I had a lot of bruising, there were no broken bones. I spent four days in hospital.

My time at Inglewood had ended.

Jackie and I were married in Brisbane two weeks later (I had to work hard to get rid of the crutches quickly). It was September 1971, and after a holiday in Sydney we went to Emerald to visit Rae and Ken. Ken had settled into life well at Emerald and he played for the local footy team. He and Rae developed lifetime friendships while living there.

Rae was due to go into hospital the day after we arrived to have her second child, who they subsequently named Troy. Ken was away working his job as a guard, so we babysat their first child, Jody. Jody's highlight for the day, after seeing his mother and new brother, was to stop at Charlie's shop for his daily ice block.

After our holiday, Jackie and I went back to Toowoomba and moved into a unit there. Shortly after we had settled in, another newly married couple from Nambour, Janelle and Keith , moved into the same block of units. Janelle and Keith had two girls, Annette and Megan, and later a son Andrew. Jackie and I became very good friends with Janelle and Keith; we spent lots of time together and shared all of our children's births.

One Saturday in Toowoomba I went to the garage where Keith worked on weekends and he showed me a stray pup. I took her home and we named her Penny. Our new arrival was the most adorable dog; she had a bulldog face that looked like she'd run into the back of a bus, but she had a very happy nature. Penny was with us for sixteen years and saw the arrival of all our children.

I did a bit more relief work around the Toowoomba district and then was sent to a small place called Nobby, a short distance from Toowoomba. This was my first relief posting as a stationmaster. To work at Nobby I had to qualify for my weighbridge ticket, as a lot of grain came into Nobby by truck for storage in the wheat silo before being sent to Brisbane by rail.

On one occasion a local farmer thought he would try to get some extra weight onto his load. When he arrived at the weighbridge I noted that in the cabin of the truck, as well as the driver, there were three other people who all stayed in the cab while it was being weighed. After the farmer had dropped off his load, there was another weigh-in. I noticed that the three people all jumped out of the cabin to make the load lighter. I advised them to get back in the cabin for correct weighing. I had paid attention to *some* things during my training.

I enjoyed my time at Nobby, learning many new things as part of my stationmaster duties. I spent about three months there before being sent to Goondiwindi as relief staff.

My leg was still a little numb after my accident at Inglewood, but the bruising had cleared up quickly. Goondiwindi was very convenient for me as I could get home to Toowoomba every weekend. It was a similar job to the one at Inglewood, but without the shunting duties. I stayed at Goondiwindi for two months, performing the duties of the permanent staff that were on leave during that time.

Jackie and I owned a Volkswagen Beetle at the time, and the window on the driver's side wouldn't close properly. I arranged to pick up a train crew at Inglewood and drop them off at Warwick on the way to Brisbane. It was the middle of winter and we were all rugged up.

After travelling for a while, a car passed us travelling at breakneck speed. Two or three kilometres further down the road, we came upon the same car. It had run off the road after colliding with a horse, that had been grazing on the side of the road. The driver told us that he was okay. The front of the car had been pushed in, but the bullbar had absorbed most of the impact. We considered ourselves lucky that the other driver had been in such a hurry; the VW would not have fared so well against the horse.

Jackie and I applied for a housing commission place in the Toowoomba area and received a house very promptly in Harlaxton, a suburb of Toowoomba. We moved in with the most basic of essentials: table, chairs, bed, one lounge, two cupboards, and a black-and-white television. Although everything we had was secondhand, we owned it all, and over time we were able to replace all the items.

After Goondiwindi I was sent to Morven, on the Charleville line west of Mungallala. It was a small town with crew quarters for one assistant and one stationmaster. The job was easy to handle and my time there went quickly.

One day I had a shunt to move a sheep wagon (known as an N-wagon) off a Charleville-bound train for delivery. N-wagons had upper and lower decks, with carriageways in between each wagon in case more than one wagon had to be loaded. The N-wagon was detached from the train and placed for unloading.

The next day, when I started duty at eight in the morning, it was pouring with rain. I rang the controller to see how the train that I had to attach the empty N-wagon to was going. He said that the train was having trouble with a hotbox on one of the loaded N-wagons.

This was a regular occurrence on the old types of wagons. After a period of travel, the bearings would become hot and eventually catch fire. The crew would pack this bearing box with oily rags and continue the journey to the next station at a slow speed.

The sheep had to be transferred to the empty wagon that I had shunted the day before. The incoming wagon was loaded with sheep, and the outgoing wagon, had now become wet and mucky in the heavy rain. All would have been well if the sheep had done the right thing and moved into the empty carriage once it was adjacent to the faulty one and the doors opened. But sheep, being sheep, don't always do what you want them to do. They needed a helping hand in the form of someone getting down on all fours and pushing them towards the doors.

I drew the short straw, but managed to get the job done. After the train departed, I was very wet, mucky and smelly, and I had to have a freezing cold shower because the boiler had not been lit yet. It took a few more showers after that to get rid of the sheep smell completely.

One type of N wagon

At Morven, there were a number of carpenters working on the goods shed. During the week they stayed in an old wooden box wagon that had been converted for the use of tradesmen. These gangs normally consisted of three men, and the box-camp wagons were fitted out with beds and a wood stove, with portable showers and toilets outside.

The wagons had wooden slats on the outside, and in wintertime they were quite uncomfortable to sleep in as the breeze blew through the slats. On weekends the tradesmen travelled back to their homes by train and returned on Monday. After the job was finished the camp wagon was transported by train to the next station.

I spent the rest of 1971 and the early part of 1972 in and around the Toowoomba area. In 1972 I applied for a position as night officer, Brisbane relief, and was successful. My time on the Toowoomba relief was over.

In 1972, Eunice and Charlie, Rae's parents, received an inheritance and purchased a house in Rockhampton; Charlie worked in the railway workshop there.

Eunice also bought a pressure cooker with some of the money. One day shortly after her purchase, she cooked corned beef for the evening meal in her new cooker. Charlie arrived home at lunchtime and after his meal he lay down for a quick nap. While he was asleep there was a heavy downpour, with lots of water flowing through the yard and under the house. The rain had stopped by the time Charlie was due to return to work, but when he got in the car it wouldn't start.

He concluded that after the downpour the spark plugs must be wet and needed drying out.

He took the spark plugs inside and put them in the small electric oven beside the pressure cooker. When the plugs were dry, Charlie was in the process of taking them out of the oven when the pressure cooker let off a burst of steam and he hit his head on the oven door. The kitchen was full of family who all erupted in laughter. Charlie was not happy with the family or the pressure cooker.

The Big Smoke and The Little Smoke

Jackie and I moved to Brisbane in 1972, and at first we had trouble finding rental accommodation due to a shortage of available properties in the city area. In the end we had to move to Redcliffe and rent a unit on a week-by-week basis until we found something more suitable for our needs.

After looking for some time, we found a house close to the railway station at Northgate.

It was a fairly rundown house, with paint peeling off the walls and a yard that was overgrown with weeds. The rent was twenty dollars a week, which was roughly one-fifth of my wages. I made a deal with the landlord that I would clean up the yard in exchange for one week's rent. I duly stacked up a big pile of rubbish for him to take away and in return our first week was free. The hot water for the house was connected to a wooden stove, which I kept supplied with wood. This turned out to be a bonus as the house was very warm in winter.

Before leaving Toowoomba, Penny had given birth to nine puppies. By the time we arrived in Brisbane we still had four left, but we managed to find homes for them within a short period of time. We still made occasional trips back to Toowoomba, where our friends, Keith and Janelle, had recently had their first child, a little girl Annette.

Jackie and I still had the old VW, but I was having daily issues with a flat battery. Every morning I had to push the car down the road to get it started. It needed a new battery, but we didn't have the money to buy one. We lived about five minutes from the station so I did most of my travelling by train.

I spent a fair bit of my time at work travelling around the suburban stations, learning the various positions there. Most stations still had individual signal cabins run by station staff, and I enjoyed the stations that had the larger cabins with up to fifty levers.

Jackie gave birth to our first child, a boy we named Keryn. Money was still a problem, so I took six weeks' leave from the railways and worked at the local Golden Circle Cannery just down the road. The work was on the production line and I was glad when my time was up, but the money sure came in handy to provide us with extras for our baby boy.

I worked at the 1973 Royal Queensland Show and found it as exciting as all the stories I had heard about over the years had led me to believe. The work wasn't difficult, but it was constant since a lot of people used train transport to get to the show. The railway staff always enjoyed the two weeks of the show, and made many trips to the Cattlemen Bar, which was close by.

I was not there in 1972, but I heard the story about Officer D, who was directing people to stand back from the edge of the platform using a hand-held speaker when he managed to walk off the edge of the platform and fall onto the tracks, much to the delight of the crowd.

In 1973, the position of assistant stationmaster, Dirranbandi was advertised. I knew the mail train ran twice a week from Brisbane to Dirranbandi and so, thinking it must be good-sized town, I applied for the job.

Nine weeks later my promotion appeared in the weekly notice: 'Assistant, Dirranbandi.' Printed in Brisbane, the weekly notice was available for viewing every Thursday. It advertised all available positions in Queensland, and also any positions that had been filled during that week. It was a must-read piece of paper for anyone seeking promotion.

I was excited to be in the stationmasters' salary grading. The leave clerk advised me that I wouldn't be taking up duties at Dirranbandi for a while because he was short of relief personnel. While waiting for my new position, I was sent to Toogoolawah to relieve, which meant I got to relive my days of working the rail motor there.

The old VW was getting harder and harder to start, so we decided to trade it in for a newer car that could make the trip out west to my new job. The Ford Falcon we purchased was about five years old and cost us two thousand dollars. I had to take out a four-year loan, but it sure was good to have a decent car. The position at

Dirranbandi included a railway house and the rent was only thirteen dollars per fortnight.

Meanwhile the leave clerk kept on putting off our departure date and so the weeks crept into months, taking us into 1974. There were many floods in the Brisbane area during that year. Just before they started, I was sent to Lowood, a station on the Toogoolawah line. Because it was raining heavily, I decided to travel to Lowood by rail motor and, after finishing my shift, catch the last goods train home.

The rain increased steadily during the night. In addition, water had been released from the Somerset Dam and this came down in great torrents. The last goods train arrived at Lowood just before midnight and it was decided that before departure the track needed to be inspected by the local ganger. When the ganger returned he advised that the water was above the level of the line and increasing rapidly. If the crew wanted to get home, he said, they had to leave immediately.

When we arrived at the affected area, the water was way above the tracks, but the crew decided it was still safe to get through. The floodwaters were making a roaring sound, and I hoped the guard's van was stable enough to get through. It turned out to be a very scary ride. I remember looking out the window of the guard's van and hearing the roar of the rushing water, realising that the train would not be able to stop. It had to keep going forward.

We eventually arrived at the Ipswich yard, and only then did we realise how much water had been allowed to come down the river from the dam. News reached us that the caravan park in Goodna, Brisbane had been washed away in the early hours of the morning by a wall of water, and many people and caravans were never recovered. In addition to this, the main rail bridge at Goodna had been washed away. The line to Brisbane was blocked and there was no way for me to get home.

I sat at Ipswich Station for most of the day, while the rain just got heavier. Finally I decided to walk out to the highway and see if I could get a lift. I stood in pouring rain for some time, soaked to the skin and very cold. I eventually managed to obtain a lift, but I felt sorry for the kind people as I dripped water all over their car floor and seat. As it happened, they were going through to Brisbane so I was able to get close to home. Huge sections of the Brisbane valley line were washed away and the branch line was closed for about nine months.

Go West Again, Young Man

Just after these floods I was given a starting date for my position in Dirranbandi. It took us quite a while to pack since we now had a lot more furniture than when we'd arrived. I purchased about eight old tea chests, which was the preferred way of packing for railway employees who were in constant movement around the state.

Our furniture was loaded into a wagon at Northgate, the doors locked and the wagon dispatched to Dirranbandi.

The estimated time of arrival was five days, which meant we could time our own arrival to reach Dirranbandi just after our furniture.

We loaded up the car, including Penny, and travelled to Dirranbandi, arriving two days after our furniture. The local work gang helped us to unload our belongings, and we provided a token of our appreciation in the form of a carton of beer for the guys to drink after the unloading had finished.

Our railway house had not been lived in for about eight months, and the lawns and gardens were overrun with weeds. The house consisted of a veranda at the front with louvre windows, and a kitchen and dining area at the back, with bathroom and toilet. The rooms were all very small. The house had a wood stove and cold running water, but there was no hot-water system.

The aboriginal meaning of Dirranbandi is 'home of frogs and waterfowl' and it certainly lived up to its name. I had never seen so many frogs. Every time we went to the toilet we had to flush before sitting down to clear the frogs out of the tank. Jackie had a phobia about frogs to start with, so this didn't help matters at all.

I was wrong about it being a reasonable-sized town. Dirranbandi had a population of about six hundred, with a bakery, hotel, cafe, shop, chemist and hospital.

During the next few months I cleaned up the house and yard, and we purchased a small portable stove and a plug-in hot-water system. The railway, at my request, sent out paint and brushes so I could spruce up all the rooms. We also purchased some seagrass matting for the floor. Finally it began to look like a home. We still had our black-and-white television, and after a while we got used to the ABC being the only television station available.

The stationmaster, Rod Witt, who had only arrived in Dirranbandi three months before me, controlled the station office, which was a separate building.

My job involved looking after the goods shed and supervising two porters. I also maintained all of the accounts pertaining to goods in and out. The accounts consisted of fifty-odd ledgers where all freight amounts were registered. The processes were all manual. At the end of the month I had to balance all the records and ledgers before sending the returns for auditing. I enjoyed the challenge this offered; each ledger contained ten or more pages and I became very proficient at balancing the books.

It was a very busy position, which I enjoyed. On some days of the week there were no train services so I had plenty of time to catch up on my bookwork.

The two porters, as well as handling all incoming and outgoing freight, also loaded wool from the carriers' trucks into wagons for despatch. All inwards and outwards freight was recorded by a system divided into four sections, and abstracts were written out for all stations to which goods were received or sent.

Jackie was settling in well and managed to find casual work at the bakery. During her working hours, the stationmaster's wife, Val, looked after Keryn.

Winter arrived quickly, and we discovered that the railway house didn't provide enough protection from the wind that blew in even when all the windows were shut.

One winter's day Keryn was rugged up in a red dressing gown and playing inside the house, which was near an open treeless paddock. He decided to do some exploring and wandered into the open paddock. When we realised he was no longer in the house, we started searching frantically out front and in the railway yard, but we couldn't see him anywhere. We were standing in the backyard looking out into the big paddock when we spotted a bit of red in the distance. I drove the car across the paddock and picked him up. We were lucky he was wearing his red dressing gown.

Dirranbandi had local football teams, with both junior and senior sides playing. The competition members, apart from us, were St George, Surat and Mungindi. I always enjoyed going to Mungindi because it was across the border and New South Wales had poker machines. We had a good mix of locals: blue-collar workers, and professionals like teachers and bank workers.

Both senior and junior sides made the 1975 grand finals played at Surat. We lost both finals, but it was a good achievement for a small town like Dirranbandi. We all felt as though we'd played our grand final a week earlier, when we'd beaten our archenemies, St George, in the semi-final.

In 1974 I was playing football every weekend. Some of the fields were regularly ploughed up and graded, and I was always playing with skinned knees. I started putting on weight and feeling unwell. I finally went to the hospital, where I was diagnosed with blood poisoning and sent to Brisbane for urgent treatment. I spent five weeks in hospital and my recovery was slow. The doctors said I was very lucky to have received treatment when I did because my blood pressure was dangerously high.

Also in 1974, there was a statewide beer strike, making beer hard to come by. The publican scouted far and wide to obtain supplies. Keg beer was out of the question as only bottled or canned supplies could be sourced. We drank quite a few horrible beers from Tasmania and South

Australia. After a couple of weeks the publican was able to source keg beer from just over the border in New South Wales. The cost was a lot higher, but the publican still made a good profit. A few months later, New South Wales had a similar beer strike and we were able to return the favour to our interstate friends.

There were a couple of local guys who used to frequent the pub, and every night they both walked home. They decided to change this habit and obtained a wheelbarrow, taking turns to push each other home on alternate nights. It got to be a joke around the town, and the police even got in on the act, telling the men they were required to have lights for their wheelbarrow. They duly obeyed, and from then on pushed each other home with a lit lantern hanging from the side of the wheelbarrow.

Our second child, Jenny, was born at Dirranbandi in 1975. Later on that year we entered Jenny and Keryn in a baby competition. Keryn took out best-baby prize and Jenny took out the best-young-baby prize. It was a marvel of modern breeding.

After a lot of complaining on my part, the railway carpenters came to our railway house and performed work on the front veranda to make it more comfortable.

Meanwhile I was having trouble with a leaking water pump in the car and decided I would fix it myself. I tightened the pump, but only succeeded in breaking the bolt in the main block. Not happy with that, I then tried to drill out the broken bolt. Soon I had a huge mess on my hands and there was no one in town qualified to fix the problem. Rod Witt and I had to make up a frame and take out the whole engine to send to Toowoomba. The problem was resolved and it only cost thirty dollars, but I gave up doing my own mechanical repairs after that.

Jackie started taking driving lessons to obtain a manual car licence as she was only licensed to drive an automatic car. She rang the town's police officer and booked in for her test. I received a call at work from the police officer asking if my wife was able to drive a car. I replied that she could. Jackie arrived home with an open licence for a bike, truck and semi-trailer—without having undertaken a driving test. Years later she was faced with having do an actual test to renew her semi-trailer licence, so she decided to cancel it.

We had been at Dirranbandi for two years when I applied for a position back at Oxley, Brisbane, and was successful. It was 1976 and my time at Dirranbandi had come to a close. I had enjoyed my position there and learned a lot. I was lucky to have had Rod Witt as my stationmaster; of all the stationmasters I've worked with, he was the best.

Oxley Station/ Redbank Roster/ Dinmore Holiday Home

Oxley Station in 1976 had a small cabin with about twelve levers. The cabin worked with Corinda and Darra stations, and in the peak hours there were two local trains that terminated at Oxley. Most of the carriages were an older type of red carriage, with a single door on either side. They were simple but good people movers.

There was one stationmaster and two assistants. It was said that the Oxley Station had been built with bricks that were used as ballast on the ships that sailed into Brisbane. There was a cattle yard in place when I first arrived, which was used for the delivery of animals by single trucks, but it was in the process of being dismantled because space was required for the construction of a bus terminal to accommodate passengers from Inala.

It was one of the best-run railway stations I had ever worked at. The stationmaster, Lex Goodwin, and the supporting staff were highly efficient.

It was also a very busy station, with a lot of ticket sales, especially on Mondays with the sale of multi-trip tickets. These tickets were pre-dated and stamped with a number every Friday to make purchases on the Monday quicker for the waiting passengers. The numbers were random and stations were advised of them every Friday. This procedure was implemented to stop passengers retaining old multi-trip tickets and reusing them the following year. At some stations, the store of multi-trip tickets had to be marked with a line going from the top left to the bottom right to stop the tickets being sold out of order by the day-relief staff. Older-type tickets made of cardboard had to be manually dated using a dating press.

Jackie and I rented a house at Goodna, which was convenient for me as I could catch a train to work when I was required to do late shifts. I was granted two weeks to learn the duties of all the positions there. The work being performed at Oxley was very different to my previous work experience.

On my second week one of the local schoolgirls poked her head in the door and asked what my name was.

Being a smarty, I replied, 'Cliff, drop over some time.'

Her name was Fiona McAlpine and she did drop over; in fact, she became the babysitter for our children. All these years later Fiona remains a very good friend of the family.

A number of Vietnamese refugee boys lived at the Wacol Migrant Camp and attended Oxley High School. I was on duty one day when a group of local lads decided to meet these Vietnamese boys at the railway station and let them know whose territory they were in. The local lads approached the Vietnamese boys on the platform and started throwing punches at them.

The Vietnamese boys looked very small in comparison to the others, but they started pulling all sorts of weapons out of their bags as if they'd been anticipating trouble. They waved their chains and knives at the local boys, who took off running in both directions along the railway tracks.

I immediately telephoned the stations on either side of Oxley and got them to stop all trains, and then I went out to restore some sort of order. I had to jump down on the tracks and stop one Vietnamese kid from slamming the head of one of the local boys onto the railway track. I told him to stop and he did so immediately, calling me 'sir' and letting the local boy get up, even though there was blood running down his own face.

Another Vietnamese boy was about to cut the ear of one of the locals with a knife. I told him to stop. He did so and I asked him what he was doing. He told me he was 'marking' the local boy and then ran away.

The melee stopped. The local boys had had enough and the police were on their way. I think the local boys learned a big lesson that day. Ironically, three weeks later the Oxley boys were at Corinda when they were threatened by local lads and Vietnamese boys came to their assistance.

I finally managed to obtain a housing commission house at Goodna. This meant cheaper rental for us. It was a fairly new home with four bedrooms, but we still had an outside thunderbox toilet because a sewerage system was not yet available in the area.

Our financial situation was still tight, and we needed to purchase carpet and mats for the house, so I decided to look for a second job. I was able to get part-time work at the Brisbane markets unloading fruit. I worked every Monday, starting at four in the morning, and also got some Sunday shifts. I did the job for eight years, and not only did it help greatly with the financial side of things, but I also enjoyed the physical part of the job as it kept me very fit.

One Monday morning at the markets I was standing next to the forklift chatting to the driver when he decided to start the forklift. My foot happened to be under the back wheel and it took the full weight of the forklift. It was very painful, but luckily I had no broken bones. It was a fair while before I could walk or get a boot on, and I was always very wary of forklifts after that.

In 1978, our second daughter, Angela, was born at the Mater Hospital in Brisbane. I attended that birth and remember it clearly; I became ill while I was watching Jackie go through labour. I think I had more nurses looking after me than Jackie did.

That year the sewerage was put through to our house, and life became much easier.

My friend Ken was successful in applying for a position as a guard on the railway at Maryborough and he purchased an old house in Fort Lane. The house required a lot of renovation, which was finally achieved over a long period of time with the help of family and friends.

I was still working at the markets when Jackie and I inspected a block of land at Redbank Plains, an area that was just starting to be developed. The block we looked at was one quarter of an acre, a fairly big block in those days. The price was $5,800, which was a lot of money for us, but we'd already decided to stay in the area because the primary school was just around the corner, and a high school was going to be built close by.

I borrowed the deposit for the land from the railway credit union and visited our block every two weeks to mow the grass. We paid our monthly mortgage for about two years and then applied for a loan to build our first house. Our loan was approved and construction started on our new house. The four-bedroom house with a HardiePlank exterior was set high on the block of land.

By 1980 projects were commencing in preparation for the Commonwealth Games in 1982, and also the Expo in 1988. Overhead wiring and all new trackwork had to be laid to accommodate the new electric trains that were being introduced for the games. This spelled the end for the local signal cabin at Oxley, as all signalling was being moved to Mayne control. It also meant a reduction in staff, with one assistant to go. As I had been the last staff member to arrive at Oxley, I decided to take up an offer to transfer as an assistant with the Redbank roster.

The roster consisted of two days at Redbank and one day each at Darra, Bundamba and Wulkuraka. At Redbank I worked one afternoon shift and one morning shift. The work consisted mainly of office work, and was constant since the Redbank stores sent all of their despatch items out by rail. On Friday morning I did the Wulkuraka shift, which was the junction for the Toogoolawah branch. It was mainly cabin work, with levers and signals. The Darra part of the roster was on Friday afternoon. This involved ticket sales and despatch of trains, as well as working the console board.

I began playing touch football with a Goodna team, and we played in the Brisbane south comp. After a few years we put together a good side and won the grand final. I continued playing touch until I was forty-six; I decided to retire when some young ones were walking faster than I was able to run.

At Redbank I met a chap I nicknamed 'Lasseter'. He was a signalman who worked a couple of days at Redbank, which still had cabins working along the Ipswich line. Lasseter was one of the few real characters I'd met on the railways. He still dressed in the uniform that had been issued to him years earlier. His shirt was so worn out that he tied a handkerchief around his neck as a collar, and most of the time he wore shoes that were so small he had to cut the backs out of them to make them fit. He drove an old Holden with door panels of different colours, and he was a frequent visitor to the Bundamba races.

> August 7th 1887.
>
> Mr. Lloyd/
>
> I want you to do <u>a bit</u> for me. I was at home sick yesterday and Price and his Ganger came to Dulbydilla and patronised the shanty, afterwards taking off their boots and having some foot races, and I was standing looking on when Mr. Hogg came along and suspended all of them and me too. I may tell you that I had not been off duty one day for the last ten years and I would not have been off yesterday only I was sick. I wish you would see Mr. Nicholson and fix matters up for me. I know you could do it if you liked. I would not ask you if Mr. Dunsmure was at home, but he is in Melbourne. I voted for him at election time. My wife is very much put out about it and she is heavy in the family way. I promise if you will do this for me it will not occur again. Let me know if you want some pumpkins.
>
> (Sgd). W.McDonald.

Early railway character

I was on duty one evening at Redbank when Lasseter hopped off the train and came into the office carrying a plastic bag, which he placed on the counter. He told me about a betting system he had been successful with, and said that in the bag were his winnings for that financial year. He said the bag contained a lot of money but he didn't know exactly how much. I asked whether he was going to put the money in the bank, but he said he was not. He told me he'd been successful with his betting system for each of the last ten years. Every year he buried his winnings in his backyard, and he was going to bury this year's winnings in the backyard as well.

Some months later I was working in a different position when I heard that Lasseter had gone fishing with his mate, and both men had fallen overboard and drowned. So, like the mystery of Lasseter's gold, I wonder if one day I'll read in the newspaper that someone digging in their backyard has discovered bundles of money. I used to say that one day I was going to find the house where Lasseter lived and buy the property, but then I wouldn't be able to call him Lasseter any more.

While at Redbank I experienced my first fatality, when someone was hit by a train while they were walking along the tracks. It was the first of many such incidents I would experience. It caused a major disruption to services and took hours to sort out.

In late 1981 I applied for a position as assistant at Dinmore. The word going around was that it would be a waste of my time because an officer from the north coast, who had a lot of seniority, was also applying for the position. The north-coast officer was duly awarded the position, but when he drove down for a look he wasn't happy with what he found and withdrew his application. As I was the only other applicant, the position was offered to me.

At Dinmore there was a siding and yards for unloading cattle. The meatworks were close by and most of the stock arrived by train. The signal cabin attached to main office had been removed and replaced by a console, which the assistants operated for shunting all stock trains, and for daily shunts of goods traffic.

There was one stationmaster, two assistants and three porters at Dinmore. It was an enjoyable job and I always referred it to as my 'holiday home'. On weekends we worked the incoming stock trains on overtime, so this position was also very good moneywise.

When things got quiet at the station, we played cricket under a large shed that was used on Fridays for dispatching goods from one of the local firms to various destinations. It was a fun time, and I'm sure people going past on the suburban trains wondered what the hell was happening. At the same time I was still playing touch football in Ipswich, so at night, if I was working, I would close up shop, play, and then return for the remainder of the shift.

In the early part of 1980 our new house was completed at a cost of $23,000, including the land, and the monthly mortgage was about $200. This was when interest rates had risen to eighteen percent. It was a difficult time, but I was lucky to be getting overtime, and I still had my earnings from the markets.

When we did get some extra money I put it into building fences, and laying cement under the house and for paths. On Fridays I purchased a six-pack and drink two each night, but sometimes I got carried away and drank the entire pack in the one session.

Our third child, Ryan, was born in 1981 at Ipswich and I was there for his birth. This time I stayed on my feet.

I thought my worst fears were coming back to haunt me when I first saw the drovers that travelled with the cattle at Dinmore. My mind went back to my days at Maryborough, when I met my first drover, but I need not have worried because these drovers were a great bunch of blokes. They would sleep in the station waiting room overnight and travel north the next day. After one of the drovers, a good friend of mine, told me he had woken one night to find someone going through his pockets, I let him camp out in the back office so he could sleep without being disturbed.

The other assistant at Dinmore was Mal Arbuthnot, a great mate to work with who came from Cunnamulla, which was as far west as it was possible to go by rail. We worked the Moura stock train that came in on Saturday evenings, but much to my chagrin they changed the arrival to fortnightly only and it was always on Mal's weekend.

We put in garden beds and planted flowers, and soon the station was looking really good. The console board was taken over by Mayne control, the main signalling hub for the whole of the suburban area of Brisbane and the north coast, including the Gold Coast. This meant we no longer did the shunting of trains and the workload became easier. We always found time to play a bit of cricket under the freight terminal shed. At Christmas, the staff celebrated with a party.

This was the now the easiest position I had worked in, and it was a great 'holiday home' for me. On most Friday nights we had a barbecue at the side of the station. On one particular Friday night, I had had three beers and was making my way home by motorcycle. Home was five kilometres away, straight down the highway. Just around the corner from the station I was pulled over by the police for a random breath test. I was wearing my railway uniform and told the officer that I'd just finished work. He said that since I'd come from work I couldn't have been drinking and sent me on my way. I made sure I was more careful after that.

I was on duty at Dinmore in 1983 when Australia won the America's Cup yacht race from the United States, and I'm sure the passengers going past must have wondered why I was waving my hands about and punching the air with my fists.

The neighbourhood at Redbank Plains was starting to get a lot more populated. When we moved there, our house was the fifth one on the block. Most of the people who lived in our area had children, and all the kids went to the same primary and high schools.

Like us, everyone was making improvements to their houses as time progressed. Over time, I'd cemented under the house, and put in an extra toilet, shower and bedroom. The backyard was also starting to improve. I'd put in a stack of old railway sleepers and constructed a terraced garden, with steps, across the back of the section. I'd also built a two-storey cubbyhouse and play area for the kids. Later on I installed another cubbyhouse in the front yard.

After a few more years, Jackie found employment as a customs officer and began work at the Brisbane airport. As our financial situation improved we were able to pay off the remainder of our mortgage. We had a new kitchen and front patio put in. We added an aboveground swimming pool to the backyard, and the trees I'd planted provided great shade. I was proud of our house and grounds.

Dinmore was a great job, but the workload was diminishing. I needed to continue my career and leave the Moura stock train to Mal. I'd been at Dinmore for seven years when I applied for a position as assistant to the Brunswick Street roster in 1988, and my application was successful.

Brunswick Street Roster

I took up my duties at Brunswick Street in late 1988, at the end of Expo 88. The expo was constructed in the inner-city area of South Brisbane, and brought to the city a new electric-train system. It was an exciting time; a lot of overseas visitors came through the station, and I enjoyed meeting them. I visited the exhibition three times, and Jackie purchased a season pass that allowed her to go many times over the six-month period.

The platforms at Brunswick, which were covered in a nonslip, brilliant white surface, were sparkling clean. The platforms were hosed and mopped every night, a task I enjoyed assisting with. The staff took pride in its maintenance, and it was the cleanest station I had ever worked at.

My roster consisted of work at Brunswick Street, Roma Street, and Pinkenba during weekdays, and Clapham Junction on Saturdays. It was a good roster, which gave me a mix of stations to work at.

I'd been at Brunswick Street for about three months when a few of the porters who manned the ticket barriers decided to test me. I got a call on the radio to say they were having trouble at the main barrier. There was a gentleman there who refused to purchase a ticket but was attempting to travel home on a train. I arrived at the barrier and saw the man standing outside the barrier. He was so big that he blocked out the light.

I approached him and asked why he was refusing to purchase a ticket. He replied that he didn't want to. I advised him that he wouldn't be travelling by train if he didn't buy a ticket. He lunged at me and started swinging punches. It was fairly easy for me to get him onto the ground just using my feet, and as he lay there

I asked again whether he would be purchasing a ticket. He replied that he would. He duly did so, and got on the next train without further incident.

On my arrival at work the next day I noticed that all the staff were very friendly towards me. I was glad that things had worked out well with the fare evader.

I witnessed my second fatality while at Brunswick Street. One day at about five in the afternoon a male person dressed only in shorts dived in front of an approaching train. It was not something we needed right on peak hour. The disruption was enormous. It was three hours before the coroner handed the track back and we were able to clear the backlog. It also affected a lot of the staff that had witnessed the incident.

The man involved had had no identification—no ticket or wallet on his person. The next day it came to light that the chap's sister had done exactly the same thing at another station at the same time of day.

The Roma Street part of the roster dealt with long-distance passenger trains, and also the trains to Sydney. At the time of the Brisbane yearly ekka, many of the passengers had to change trains at Roma Street and this meant the platforms became clogged up. Part of our job was to get the passengers to move away from the stairs once they'd stepped onto the platform.

One of the other assistants at Roma Street was another railway character. He was nicknamed 'Chips' and I was amazed at his ability to handle crowds. One day, when I was having trouble moving a group of people, during the Ekka, who wouldn't listen to me, Chips grabbed the portable speaker and asked them to move further along the platform. When there was no response he yelled into the speaker, 'You with the fat stomach, please move away from the stairs.'

Many of the individuals in the group fell into this category, and they *all* started to move away. It was not something I was ever game to repeat.

Rae and Ken sold their house at Fort Lane in 1989 and moved into a nice home in Torquay, which is part of Hervey Bay. In 1990, the guard positions in Maryborough were retrenched, which meant that for Ken to continue employment with the railways he and Rae would have to move to Brisbane. Instead, Ken resigned and purchased a bread run, which meant they could continue to live in Hervey Bay.

I enjoyed my rostered day at Pinkenba. It had a large shunting yard that provided services from various sidings, which included the shipping of all fuel for west and north Queensland, and grain coming in from the west. The number of movements of grain over the next six months slowed down, as it was a very bad year for wheat crops. Over the next few years the fuel movements also slowed down due to the shift from train to road transport. Eventually, within three years, the whole yard closed and the staff moved to other areas.

The best shift of all for me was Clapham Junction. Clapham was the transhipping yard for fruit being transported from the north to the south, and it also handled the Nitro Phil trains that travelled from Newcastle to the northern mining areas. In addition, there were daily car wagons transporting new cars from the south.

Clapham Shunting yard was a dual-gauge yard, with separate shunt engines and shunters for both systems. The shunting staff had to be qualified in both gauge systems. Clapham handled fully laden fruit trains from the north en route to the southern markets.

The whole system of shunting has changed significantly from the way it used to be. Shunters nowadays work much more safely because all wagons have auto couplers and shunters are not required to get in between the wagons. Two-way radios are also used now, giving the shunters direct contact with the shunt driver.

The shunters main task now entails attaching and detaching wagons that make up outgoing services, and shunting incoming traffic into various sidings. Shunters are also trained in the testing of a train before departure. This involves ensuring that all running parts are in place. They do an air test at the back of the train by releasing air from the brake system and then have the driver recharge the airlines.

Back then, when trains were sent south they were restricted to half the length of the Queensland trains, which meant that twice the number of trains was sent south. In the 1980s, the fruit was shipped in containers, making it easier to tranship. Prior to container traffic, transhipping was done manually. Staff transferred goods by wheelbarrow between wagons positioned on either side of the platform.

The staff employed to do this tranship work on weekends consisted of anyone who required some extra cash and was willing to turn up and work. One story doing the rounds at the time was that the police turned up at the station one day looking for a certain person of interest, and half of the workers bolted. When this manual system ceased, crews switched to unloading all container traffic using an overhead crane.

When I was at Clapham, every Saturday a car would pull up outside, and the driver would beep his horn and wait for me to come out of the office and acknowledge him.

At first I was confused, and wondered who this person was. I asked the staff if they knew him, and learned that he was one of the managers who had devised an ingenious way of increasing his pay packet. He drove through the yard every Saturday, and then on Monday booked in four hours' overtime for a callout. In all the times I saw this man, he never got out of his car once.

There was a crew on duty at Clapham that used to drive the new cars off the car wagons from the south for transport elsewhere. The car wagons had to be inspected on arrival and each car was gone over for shortages. Most of the items taken were spare tyres and car radios. There were occasions when every car was broken into. One day the temptation became too much for one fellow, and he kept on driving—out the gate and on down the road. He didn't realise, however, that the new cars had minimal fuel in the tanks and his 'escape vehicle' soon ran out of petrol.

One of the jobs in Clapham yard was to clean the points in the shunting yard. Sand was pumped onto the tracks when a driver wanted to stop with a big load. The cleaning of points required a long-handled scraper to clear this loose sand from the blades, and a brush to apply oil to the points so they operated properly. If the points were not cleaned and oiled, they could remain half cocked after a shunt trailed through. If that happened, the next facing diesel would derail after going through the half-cocked points. This was the cause of most derailments in shunting yards.

One staff member, whose duties involved cleaning the points in the shunting yard, had a sleep disorder. He frequently fell asleep on the job, then woke up a few seconds later and continued his work. All the staff knew of his condition and kept watch over him. Sometimes when this chap nodded off, the shunt had to stop and wait for him to wake up and continue his cleaning. Eventually the staff agreed that he might be better suited to a different position.

Once there was an audit being undertaken on the usage of diesel fuel by the shunts and working diesels, and what went through the gauges. A discrepancy of ten thousand litres was discovered. Further investigation was undertaken, but no reason could be found for the shortfall and it was officially put down to a bad leakage. Coincidentally, most of the staff had hobby farms that used diesel-powered machinery. We concluded that the bad leak must have repaired itself as no more shortfalls were reported after that.

When Christmas approached, the staff decided they would decorate the office building with toilet paper, and they wrapped the paper around the front of the building facing the main line. On the arrival of the Sydney to Brisbane mail train the next morning, the staff assembled on the platform, stood to attention and saluted as the train passed through. That little stunt meant another appearance before management with the invitation to 'please explain'.

The most important person in the big shunting yards was the number taker; a good number taker was essential for the yard to operate efficiently. This individual's job was to collect all information concerning wagon consignees for incoming trains, and document this information for passing onto the shunters so they could perform their shunts. It also applied to traffic coming out of sidings for transit south. Number takers also compiled the outgoing lists for train crews.

While I was at Clapham there was talk of the introduction of a new computer-based system called 'yard control'. The wagons would arrive in the yard via computer and would then be shunted from road to road. In addition, lists for all outgoing trains would be compiled and dispatched by computer. The yard foreman would operate the computer, and this meant the demise of the number taker's job.

All yard staff, including supervisors, were required to attend a yard-control training course for one week to learn about the new computer system. It was a very difficult time since many of the older staff had very few, if any, computer skills.

The new system was duly introduced, but it took a few months for most yards to become comfortable with it. A few wags tampered with the keyboards and swapped some of the keys around, totally frustrating the operator. I saw many keyboards flying through the air during this period.

A few years after that, Clapham became a Queensland-only yard, and was transformed into a holding yard for Acacia Ridge traffic only. The unfortunate effect of this decision was that no standard-gauge roads were retained at Clapham. One of the last relief staff to work at Clapham was Barry Tait, who i first met at Amby in 1970.

The movement of fruit from the north by rail gradually diminished, and then it was switched over to road freight. Most of the other traffic also decreased in Acacia Ridge and this saw the eventual closure of the yard for transhipping purposes.

Brisbane Relief / Acacia Ridge

In the middle of 1990, the duties of my roster job were reviewed. Because of the relief duties at Roma Station, it was decided that the position needed to be upgraded. When this happened and the position was advertised, I was not successful in winning it.

I applied for a position as stationmaster fourth-class Brisbane relief and was successful. The job was then split up into two separate positions: city relief and freight relief. I made the decision to move to freight relief, which meant I would work at freight yards only.

My last relief job on the city trains was at Darra, relieving the stationmaster. One of my staff there was a lad porter called Peter. Peter had a bad habit of standing behind me every time I opened my lunch to eat on my break. When he left there was always a bad smell remaining. It got so bad that I had to lock myself in the ticket office to eat lunch.

One day a woman came to the office wringing wet, and she told me the roof in the subway was leaking. I went off to have a look at the area, suspecting a cracked water pipe, but I found Peter hosing the subway roof. I gave him the rounds of the kitchen.

On another occasion I asked Peter to go over to the cement factory, where staff from Darra shunted wagons for outgoing bags of cement, and counted the total number of frames and tarps on hand for covering the cement wagons. It was midday when Peter went, and he still hadn't returned when I went home at two. I found out the next day that he'd been away for three hours.

I was glad to be rid of Peter when my time at Darra was finished, but little did I know what lay ahead.

In the early 1990s, all members of staff were called to attend an important meeting. At the meeting, management advised us that from a certain date the railway as we knew it would be split into four different sections, each one of which would be run by a separate manager.

The section where I was to work was yards and freight. It was the end of the mateship railway that I had experienced to date, and it eventually pitted mate against mate. It was also announced that stationmasters' positions in charge of yards would no longer exist. From then on, managers for yards would be drawn from the drivers' ranks. I remember thinking at the time that this system wouldn't work out because stationmasters were far more experienced in yard operations than train drivers.

The old system of promotion was also changed, going from a seniority-based system to a merit-based one. I totally agreed with this change, as I had experienced a number of cases where people had ended up in unsuitable positions solely on the basis of long-term employment with the railway. As I found out after this system was implemented, it only worked if proper protocols were put in place and adhered to. Interview panels consisted of a chairperson, a content person and an HR person. There were times when I saw these panels manipulated to suit certain candidates.

I was advised that I would be going to Acacia Ridge to relieve in the near future. I had heard a lot of comments about Acacia Ridge, which I knew was a large yard with over one hundred staff.

I took up my relief position at Acacia Ridge in 1992 and set about learning how the yard operated. It was a massive change for me, as I'd never worked with the systems in operation there before. Most of the shunting staff had come from Roma Street yard after its closure.

The complex consisted of an interstate terminal for container traffic, an interstate yard for shunting, and a Queensland yard for northbound trains. There was still a standard-gauge shunt operating on all of the sidings throughout the yard.

Working at Acacia Ridge was Vic, the talkative fellow from Roma Street yard who walked around all day carrying a brown envelope. He had already insinuated himself into a cushy job that required very little of his precious time.

Also under supervision at Acacia Ridge were the shunting staff, who were divided between standard gauge and Queensland. There was a yard foreman on each shift as well as foreman shunters out in the shunting yard. Shunting gangs started out consisting of three men, but these gangs eventually went down to two men when two-way radios were introduced for all shunting jobs.

The assistant controlled all operations from an office in the main building, including interaction between firms and shunters. I'd always admired the person performing the duties of the assistant, as there was immense pressure on them at various times. I knew it was going to take me a long time to master this position, but I was keen to achieve that level of competency. I was given plenty of time to get to grips with the operation, but I realised that the only way to succeed was to get into the chair, make my mistakes and learn from them. Well, I did make plenty of mistakes, but as time went on they became fewer and fewer.

There was a vacancy at Acacia Ridge and my manager told me I stood a good chance of obtaining the position if I applied. I did, was successful, and in 1993 I was classified as assistant, Acacia Ridge. I was still having problems running the yards efficiently, and my manager pointed out to me that he might have made a mistake. My only excuse was that I was a slow learner, but I was determined to succeed eventually.

The interstate container terminal was put up for tender in the hope of finding a private buyer. One buyer was successful, and a lease was drawn up for the company to run the terminal and all shunting on the standard-gauge operations. As it turned out, there was a huge mistake made in the wording of the lease, and years later it came to light that there was no third-party access available for a train from the south into the standard-gauge yard.

It also meant that more than half the staff would not be required at Acacia Ridge since the railways would be handling Queensland traffic only. Most of the shunting staff ended up in positions in the main office in town. As time went by, they ended up having good skills required for a number of the positions.

Due to the changes, the position of assistant at Acacia Ridge became a lot easier than in the past, and eventually all the office staff were moved on. The Queensland yard was fully wired to accommodate electric locomotives into the yard to haul the northbound trains.

The new firm running the standard-gauge terminal was earmarked to take over the office space from us assistants, and we were to move to a small office out of the way until another office could be built near the Queensland yard.

The long-time manager at Acacia Ridge, Jim Mahon, retired and was replaced by John, who had previously worked as yard foreman at Clapham Junction.

I got a huge surprise when starting duty one Monday. There to greet me was Peter, my lad porter from Darra, who had been reassigned from the city network to work at Acacia Ridge. Initially his duties consisted of office cleaning, but then he was given the job of cleaning the three electric locomotives that were required as freight trains each day. The work included sweeping the cab and toilets, and mopping the floors, a fairly simple set of tasks that even Peter could manage easily. After a while, however, he decided that there was an easier way of doing things, and began hosing out the cab to streamline the operation.

Peter's new method of cleaning was discovered by an outgoing driver who, when he sat in his seat, found himself in a pool of water. Peter had claimed another victim with his water mishaps.

He was moved on once again to another position, this time cleaning points in the shunt yard. Cleaning points was another job that was simple to perform, and Peter enjoyed the freedom he had to move about the yard. Over time his mishaps diminished and he stopped drawing as much attention—until the day he came into the office at eight pm, three hours after his shift had ended. He said that he had lain down under a tree to rest and fallen asleep. He asked if he could book the three hours as overtime. I decided then that it was time for Peter to move on.

In 1994 Jackie and I decided that, since our son Ryan was our only child still at school, it was time to move house.

The neighbourhood at Redbank Plains had changed quite a lot and many of our original neighbours had moved on. We looked at a house at Birkdale that was one street back from the water, but it needed a lot of renovation work. It was a double-storey brick house with a double garage. We purchased the house for $158,000 and rented it out for twelve months while we were still living at Redbank Plains. We put the house at Redbank Plains on the market, but finding a buyer proved to be difficult.

We travelled to Maryborough in 1993 for Rae and Ken's twenty-fifth wedding anniversary. It was a surprise party, and everybody had a great weekend. All the Scougall family was present, and that night they performed their favourite song 'I'm a Little Teapot'. At the party, Jackie and I noticed that our daughter Jennie was keeping close company with Rae's son Troy, who was stationed with the armed forces in Katherine, Northern Territory.

Ken's bread run wasn't producing enough money, and he'd been putting in very long hours just to get by. He decided to sell the run, and in 1994 took up a position at a sawmill in Maryborough. He went on to build his and Rae's dream house in Banana Street, Granville.

We were still living in Redbank Plains when our daughter Jennie presented us with our first grandchild in 1995. She was a beautiful baby named Hope, and we looked forward to spending time with her. Both mother and baby lived with us in the rooms on the ground floor of our house. It was lovely having our little 'Sparkle' so close to us.

We had another surprise when Troy turned up at our house for a visit. Jackie and I thought it strange to see him, but it turned out that he and Jennie had kept in contact while he was in Katherine. There were even more surprises in store for us. Jennie informed us that she would be moving to Katherine with Hope.

We were very sad to have our daughter and grandchild leave, and what's more, to a place so far away, but Jackie visited them after they'd moved to Katherine and we also spent lots of time in contact via Skype. Later on Troy was transferred, and he and Jennie moved to Newcastle. In 1998 we travelled to Newcastle for the arrival of our second grandchild, Taylah, another beautiful baby girl.

Acacia Ridge New building

The new building at Acacia Ridge was approaching completion and eventually the staff moved in. We had total visibility over the main shunting yard. The whole working environment had now changed for the better, and all the faults that we had once had to tolerate were now gone.

We were called to a staff meeting and informed that the supervisor's position had been reviewed. In addition, the assistant's position had been abolished and replaced by the position of area coordinator. This meant that, once more, I would have to apply for the new position.

Nine coordinator positions had been created, with four located at Acacia Ridge and four at Normanby, with one relief position to cover all leave. I was lucky enough to win one of the positions at Acacia Ridge. Three of my workmates from the old yard, Richard, Keith and Darryl, filled the other three positions.

At Acacia Ridge we were responsible for the yards at Redbank, Dinmore and Clapham. The Normanby coordinators looked after Bindha and Pinkenba branches. It was an exciting time, as we had to start from scratch in formulating work procedures to control those other yards.

The complex at Acacia Ridge was unique in that it was the first yard to accommodate shunters and running men in the same amenities building. There were some concerns that things might not work out between the two groups, but as time passed no problems arose. In the following few months, the coordinators also took on responsibility for refuelling and cleaning all the diesels at Acacia Ridge. Previously this had been done at Fisherman Island.

At Acacia Ridge there were two shunts working simultaneously at either end of the yard. One shunt made up the sets for northbound trains at that end. These trains consisted of QLX box wagons, and were placed in various roads in the shed for loading. The night-shift crew performed this shunting. Eventually the QLX wagons were phased out and replaced by containers loaded at a terminal set up on the side of the goods shed. When the phasing out was complete, only one shunt was required after that.

My acting manager, John was required to relieve in Brisbane for a three-month period and he asked whether I would be willing to act as manager while he was away. I readily accepted as I had a pretty good knowledge of the areas covered by the manager's position. The manager controlled all staff at Gympie, Maryborough West, Bundaberg and all stations on the Monto line.

There was still much to be done in the planning of the marshalling of northbound trains. The terminal at Acacia Ridge was supposed to work as both train-into siding and train-out of-siding. This would only work efficiently if more room were made available to accommodate the full trains in and out. Examination of trains was to be done on arrival in the terminal sidings.

There was an added problem. If any defect wagons were found during the examination, they had to be cut out. Eventually the examiners refused to test the inbound trains in the terminal, so all trains had to be received into the yard before being shunted into the terminal.

Health-and-safety regulations dictated that the yard had to be audited on a regular basis and all employees screened during this process. Safety in the workplace was now a high-agenda item at all staff meetings. Monthly health and safety meetings were held, and all employees at Acacia Ridge were represented. One agenda item raised at every meeting was the importance of all yards being alcohol free.

One night, when I was acting manager, I took a phone call from Keith, the area coordinator on duty, who advised me that a member of the shunting gang had appeared for work in an unfit condition. When I approached the shunter, I could smell alcohol on his breath. I didn't have the authority to suspend him, but I advised the manager above me, who did. After further investigation, the shunter was discharged from employment. It was a defining moment, as the incident sent an important message to the rest of the employees that new standards were now in place.

Ken Tate was appointed to manager Acacia Ridge in 1998 after his position at Maryborough was abolished. As coordinators, we worked well with Ken and a good relationship was developing.

My friend, Col McCarthy, was a shunt driver at Acacia Ridge. He and I started making yearly trips to a touch footy carnival run by the railways, held at various towns throughout the state. It was always a great time away and most of the team were part of the shunting grade at Acacia Ridge. We made the trips in a hire vehicle that seated thirteen people. Col and I organised the whole trip, including booking accommodation and obtaining necessary supplies.

One of these trips was to Rockhampton. We all met at Acacia Ridge at six am, and loaded up the bus with everything we needed to reach Rocky. I was the nominated driver, and before we left I laid down the law about drinking and unruly behaviour, and I also stressed that there was to be no smoking of dreadful green weed in my bus. Off we went. The bus hadn't even reached the end of the driveway before I got a whiff of pungent smoke. So much for the stern lecture.

Our footy team was a thirsty lot. Col had brought along a guitar and there was a lot of drinking, singing and laughter going on at the back of the bus. After about three hours of driving there were a number of pit-stop requests. I pulled the bus over to the side of the highway and ten guys got out, lined up and began relieving themselves at the side of the road. It was my time for revenge.

I took off and parked the bus fifty metres down the highway. I sat there listening to the passing traffic acknowledge our fellows with beeps of their horns. The pit stops became more and more frequent as the trip progressed, and I employed the same procedure at every stop.

As for our ability to play touch footy, our guys should have should stuck to drinking. We attended four carnivals and received the wooden spoon at two of them, but I know that of all the teams that participated we had the best time of all. I still give big thanks to Col for these footy memories.

Redbank was originally set up for the storage of coal wagons, but this facility was soon transferred to Fisherman Island and the staff at Redbank moved on to other positions. Redbank was then used for wagon storage only.

The coordinators from Normanby were moved to Fisherman Island, where they controlled that yard and the console board for the yard. There were still employees at Normanby to handle the workings and storage of livestock wagons after unloading at Dinmore. Yards at Bindha, Pinkenba and Wacol were also closed.

The only yards left operating in the Brisbane area were Fisherman Island, Acacia Ridge, Clapham and Normanby. Moolabin, which was still in operation, was being managed by shunting staff and one stationmaster.

Electric locomotives were relocated from Brisbane to work on the northern coal traffic, and they were replaced by 2800-class diesels. Staff from Maryborough operated the trains in and out of Acacia Ridge. Some of the lad porters who had once worked with me were now train drivers at Maryborough.

At Acacia Ridge, we took over responsibility for the rosters that had previously been handled by a roster clerk. Clapham yard was redeveloped and restricted to Queensland gauge only. It was set up as a working yard with a temporary office and a shunt crew from Acacia Ridge, which worked the two trains daily that were bound for the west.

This arrangement was in operation for a period of two years until the western traffic eventually ceased and the Clapham shunt crew finished up. It allowed us to use Clapham for the storage of container wagons, and Acacia Ridge shunters could now work the stock trains. Staff members at Normanby were relocated to other positions.

Ken was still working for the sawmill in Maryborough in early 1998, but I knew he missed his former job as a shunter. I made a successful appeal to Ken Tate on my friend Ken's behalf, and was able to tell Ken that a position could be made available for him if he wanted to make the move. After a few days Ken contacted me again and said he would accept. It was a very big decision for him and Rae. I knew how much they loved their new house, and if things didn't work out I could be in trouble.

After Ken completed his catch-up training, he moved to Brisbane and commenced work at Acacia Ridge as a shunter. Rae followed at a later date, and they sold their dream home at Maryborough. For some time I felt a sense of guilt about this. After several moves within the Brisbane area, they finally decided on a house in Prince of Wales Parade in Alexandra Hills. The penalty for my part in their new circumstances was to carry their very heavy dining table up and down many flights of stairs.

Ken enjoyed being back in the role of shunter, but he realised that he only had about ten years of working life left so he was investigating various options to progress his career. After some time he was successful in applying for a tutor position at Acacia Ridge.

Acacia Ridge took over the maintenance of the end-of-train signals that were required on the rear of all trains, maintenance previously carried out by the staff at Normanby before its closure. The signals were required to show a red light at night, and maintenance consisted of replacing old batteries and blown bulbs.

In 2003 my manager, Ken Tate, accepted the offer of an early retirement package and finished up.

The position for a replacement was advertised and I applied for it. In the lead-up to interviews, however, I withdrew my application because I was not happy with some of the pre-selection processes.

The position was filled by Barry , who came out of the driver's grade, and he took up duties three weeks later. I was not bitter about missing out on the job, and I looked forward to forming a good working relationship with him. As time passed, however, there seemed to be a lack of communication happening between the new manager and the area coordinators, who were becoming more isolated. I tried to stimulate the communication by suggesting that the manager address the coordinators on a daily basis, which would enable us to keep him informed of any relevant issues that arose.

This arrangement was put into place, but it didn't last long. Sometimes days and weeks passed without any contact between the parties concerned, and this was a hindrance to the efficient operation of the complex.

My nemesis, Peter, was now confined to cleaning duties only. Every Monday I drove around and inspected the other yards under our control. On one of these occasions, one of the shunters played a trick on Peter by getting him to sit in my chair and assume the position of area coordinator. The shunter then went downstairs and rang Peter, telling him there was a wagon of birds at Clapham with the door open and that birds were flying everywhere.

On my arrival back at Acacia Ridge, I saw Peter walking briskly up the road. When I asked where he was going, he said he was heading to Clapham to shut the door on the wagon with the birds in it. I had to reprimand the shunter for his antics.

Eighteen months later, Peter got into a ruckus in the amenities room and eventually was sacked for throwing a punch. My time with Peter had finally come to an end.

Vic, the brown-paper-envelope man, had continued in his excellent working situation. His main job for the day was to take correspondence to, and pick up mail from, the main office in town, and also perform a runaround, picking up any items required for Acacia Ridge.

Vic had decided to commence his duties at four am and finish his shift at midday. This worked out well for him because none of the offices in town opened until nine am. This left him with plenty of time to conduct the main part of his work, which was talking, something he was very proficient at. Eventually Vic retired, but, strangely enough, his vacant position was never filled.

The Final Stop

In 2005 manager Barry advised me that he'd been seconded to head office and that I would be relieving for him in his absence. I was delighted with the prospect of new challenges ahead. I was given use of a railway car, and the increase in salary was comparable to shift-work wages earned by area coordinators.

Over a period of eight years, I renovated our house at Birkdale. I completely repainted the interior, sanded back and painted the original wooden floor, erected a new deck in the backyard, and built an extra room downstairs with a toilet and shower. I also completely renovated the upstairs bathroom.

In addition, the exterior of the house was rendered and painted, and the roof sprayed. The old patio, which had been enclosed, was opened up and railings put in place with new steps and door. We also had a swimming pool installed in the backyard. Jackie and I put the house on the market in 2005. It took six weeks to sell, and made us a nice profit. We then purchased a single-storey four-bedroom house on a small block in Alexandra Hills.

In 2005 Ken applied for a position as coordinator at Coppabella and was successful. He and Rae relocated to a railway house there, and as with all railway houses there was a lot of cleaning to be done before they could move in.

Queensland Railways performed a review and released a draft document called 'Freight 2004', which outlined the future of freight and yards in the Brisbane area. Even though these suggested changes involved a lot of work, I was confident that I could adapt. One of the changes was that management of the complex at Moolabin was to be gradually handed over to private industry over a period of approximately six months. The handover was to be undertaken train by train, and as this occurred staff would be moved to Acacia Ridge to make up for short staffing there. The ballast wagons that worked out of Normanby were to be relocated to Clapham, and this service operated by shunters from Acacia Ridge.

After all the changes were made, all freight operations in the Brisbane area would be conducted at Acacia Ridge and Fisherman Island. Normanby would still be used for storage of excess container wagons during the Christmas period.

The butt-weld complex handled lengths of rail received from the south by rail and transhipped through Acacia Ridge to Bindha for joining. These finished rails were later dispatched by rail to northern destinations for use in projects. Staff from Acacia Ridge carried out this work. There were future plans to relocate this complex into a new facility at Clapham. This would make the new complex more accessible from Acacia Ridge.

We had ten years with our first two granddaughters, and then in 2006 our daughter Angela presented us with our first grandson, Morgan. He had beautiful ginger hair just like Granny. In 2007, Angela gave birth to a daughter called Katherine, who had beautiful blonde hair. The next year, Angela's second son was born. He was named Flynn and he had brownish hair that was close to being ginger.

In 2007, Ken moved from Coppabella after promotion to AO5 controller in Mackay. I was very pleased for him; he was now a level above my classification and had achieved this in a very short amount of time.

Queensland Rail was holding talks about the running of interstate freight trains from Melbourne into Acacia Ridge. However, there had been no discussion on an agreement for the method of movement of trains into Acacia Ridge standard-gauge yard. Because of the difference in gauge, the only possible movement from the main line to a standard-gauge siding was via a road two hundred and forty metres in length. This meant that the maximum number of wagons that could be handled at one time was eleven.

This operation went ahead, but the reduced level of traffic was not enough to maintain a viable profit. The ideal place for the storage and shunting of these wagons would have been Clapham, but it hadn't rated a mention five years earlier.

Talks had taken place with the operator of the standard-gauge complex to allow third-party access to that yard. The service was to have been called Interrail, but agreement between the two parties was contested through the courts and ended up taking years to sort out.

Following meetings to discuss the running and storage of this train, it was decided that work would go ahead. The service could access an area at the northern end of the yard, with facilities to tranship and store twelve hundred metres of rolling stock. The changes meant that a new set of points and controlling levers had to be installed in the area at the northern end of the yard. The admittance shunting and dispatching of this service was to be carried out by staff from Acacia Ridge. The Interrail train could now start running at a profit because of its ability to operate a longer service.

At the same time a service called the Great South Pacific Express (GSPE) was being implemented. This beautifully crafted train was constructed by staff at the Townsville workshops, and was a remarkable achievement by the woodworking craftsmen. The woodwork was of a dark oak colour, and the decor in the sitters and sleeping cars had an oriental theme. After a number of meetings, it was decided that this new train would be bogie-transhipped at Acacia Ridge. One of the ideas put forward was that special track be laid at Acacia Ridge to either increase or decrease the specially made bogies the train ran on over this section.

I thought this idea had merit since the track could be also used for freight services that normally had to be transhipped at Acacia Ridge, but this was a very costly exercise and other options were considered.

The government at the time decided to go ahead with manual transhipping. This system was very labour intensive as forty-seven staff had to be used, and in addition to this, passengers had to lay over in Brisbane for twelve hours. Eventually the system was modernised to a version that used fewer staff.

When this train did commence operation, I loved walking through each of the carriages and the sleeping car while the train sat at Acacia Ridge. The service was implemented to promote tourism, with many visitors originating from America. The service was fully booked when it commenced operation, and it ran from Sydney to Cairns return.

The whole concept was ahead of its time, but after eighteen months' operation the United States was rocked by a financial crisis and the number of overseas passengers dropped dramatically. To maintain the service as a viable proposition, it was opened up to the local market at a cheaper rate. Even at this cheaper rate, the service failed to make a profit and eventually the service was cancelled and the carriages stowed away. They would later be sold to overseas interests.

In my duties as acting manager, I was kept very busy. Medicals for the shunting-grade staff had been allowed to slip and many were nearly out of date. These medical examinations were required to be taken yearly as part of the certification process for our major shunting complex. It took a lot of time to achieve, as working rosters had to be changed to accommodate the unavailability of staff. At times, overtime was required.

After my time as acting manager, I went back to my old position of area coordinator. I enjoyed the less-busy working environment, although communications were still an issue with the manager. Barry appeared to be building an empire by creating additional positions under his control, but in many cases the appointed staff were clearly not required.

At Acacia Ridge, the coordinators worked their shifts with the same foreman. When the coordinators took leave, the foremen performed the relief duties. One of our foremen was promoted to a position in Brisbane and the vacant position was advertised in the weekly gazette. One of the applicants, a woman named Denise Hookey from Cloncurry, was the successful applicant. There was talk between the coordinators about who would accept her as their foreman and I volunteered.

Denise was the first female foreman in Brisbane freight yards, and I was immediately amazed at her management skills, especially since she was not yet thirty years of age. She was excellent in handling the staff, and her general demeanour and work ethics were very good. I wished I had had that kind of ability at such a young age, and I knew she would go onto bigger and better things.

I was only too happy to work with someone like Denise in my last few years with the railways. I was able to hand over the reins to someone with a lot of ability. Denise always listened to any advice I gave her, and her management skills were improving all the time. We got on very well, and we got through the work with a lot of laughter as well. It reminded me of my happy times at Mayne Junction.

A new position was created called senior area coordinator. It was an acting position only and was never advertised through the weekly notice. Arthur was appointed to this role. It was a position one level above the area coordinators, and I always thought it was created as part of my manager's empire-building exercise. All communication to and from the manager had to be directed through the senior area coordinator. This was very disappointing, and to me it seemed like a waste of resources.

There were no specific duties for the new position, but as time went on the occupant took on any new, miscellaneous jobs. It was obvious to me that the coordinators were becoming more and more isolated from management. I thought I'd seen the last of brown-envelope-carrying employees, but now we had two more of them.

As time progressed I felt that any accolades for good work performed were being attributed to persons other than the ones who had actually done the work. The coordinators at Fisherman Island and also Acacia Ridge, were a real credit to the organisation in achieving the end result without any manager imput.

The area coordinators all had a good working relationship with the controlling supervisors in Brisbane, and the employees involved with movement of freight in and out of Brisbane.

I got on really well with the diesel clerk, Geoff, who knew where every diesel was supposed to be operating. Sometimes, when he was travelling on the train to work and spotted a diesel out of place, as soon as he arrived at work he would place a phone call to organise relocation to the correct spot. We always joked that one day we would both get our picks and shovels and do a bit of digging in our old mate Lasseter's backyard in Ipswich.

I nicknamed Geoff 'Baby' because he started every conversation with 'Baby ...'. It was always good to chat to Geoff; our conversations always ended in laughter.

Advice was relayed to us that the area coordinators would be taking over the running of the Fisherman Island complex as well as Acacia Ridge. There was to be no upgrade in classification despite the added responsibilities. The area coordinators went to Fisherman Island and underwent training in their systems.

We were earmarked to take control of the staff at Fisherman's Island to provide them with shift handovers and any necessary assistance during their shifts. The Fisherman Island coordinators would be moved over to a different section that controlled the local operating panel for points and signals, but they had no responsibility for the freight movements. Not all the area coordinators saw this as a good move as there was too much transport involved.

When the time came for us to take over the complex at Fishermans Island, I advised management that I wouldn't be taking on the additional responsibilities as part of my duties. The changed arrangements were shelved and we went back to the existing working environment, with the Fisherman Island coordinators retaining total control of the freight operations.

Over the next few years, container traffic to the north began to decrease as the private firm at Moolabin began to gather more traffic. The Interrail service had won its court case and gained full access to the standard-gauge yard at Acacia Ridge. This meant longer trains could be managed in that yard.

With all the changes that had gone on, the duties of the coordinators had decreased and I had become very disillusioned with the management at Acacia Ridge. I made a decision to take six months' leave and see how I felt about coming back after that. During this time Denise was to relieve in my position as coordinator.

It became even worse when the manager raised the classification level of one of the brown-envelope carriers. This then put the position at the same level as the area coordinators, even though the workload was diminishing. It had the approval of higher management, which was even more disappointing.

The *Final* Final Stop

I did return from leave, but my morale was still low, and even my work was not enough to keep me happy since the workload had decreased even further in my absence. It was getting to the stage where the area coordinator's position needed to be downgraded.

I approached my manager with a proposal that the position should be downgraded, and the current area coordinators offered a redundancy package. I offered to make the changes that would be required if my proposal was adopted.

My proposal was accepted. My work for the changed arrangements involved the creation of rosters to accommodate five yard coordinators who would work five days in seven, and included Sundays as part of the roster. In addition, the rosters would have to fit in with the new fade system, where only a certain number of night shifts could be worked in a row.

I put together the rosters over a three-week period and presented them to staff for appraisal and comment. All went well, and I worked on for a more few weeks. On 16 April 2010 I signed off duty for the last time after forty-five years of service.

Ken was moved to Jilallan for a short while, and then moved back to Mackay. He finished work on 23 December 2012. He and Rae retired to Hervey Bay, where they now live in their second dream home. They make regular trips to Newcastle to visit their other son Jody, and their grandchildren Keira and Jay.

It has been an incredible journey for two little lad porters from Maryborough. Between us, we put in eighty-five years of service to Queensland Railway.

Throughout my career I often thought about what it must have been like for the railway men in the early

1900s in the steam era with only basic resources to deal with. The conditions they had to put up with must have been terrible, working the steam locomotives in pouring rain with wind blowing in their faces as they poked their heads out looking for a small flicker of light that would show the position of the approaching signal. Those steam-train crews sometimes cooked the meat for their evening meal on the same shovel they used to load coal into the burner by holding the shovel over the flames. The early station staff also did the hard work so that we, at a later time, could enjoy the benefits of a great job.

After seeing a lot of branch lines close down, I often thought of the men who laid the tracks, and the women who travelled with their husbands and lived in tents alongside the track, even growing their own fresh vegetables. All these people provided a great platform for my generation to carry on with and I feel great gratitude towards them.

I was extremely lucky to enjoy a wonderful working life with Queensland Railway and thoroughly enjoyed my experiences. I was lucky to have met and worked with a number of really good mates, and throughout my working life had many moments of excitement. I made many deserved friends, but I did not suffer fools well. My son Keryn has carried on part of the family tradition and is employed as a train controller at Mayne.

I have always believed that it's not where you start, but where you finish that matters. I had aspired to achieve a position as assistant in the suburban area, and I managed to reach the top of that grade during my career. I'm very proud of what the area coordinators at Acacia Ridge achieved. It could not have been done without the help of the coordinators from Fisherman Island.

I also think back to some of the low moments in my career and regret that the breakup of the system into four parts in the 1990s was the start of the dog-eat-dog system that exists today, but I guess it was inevitable.

The most disturbing incident during my career occurred while I was at Acacia Ridge. The acting manager called me into the signal cabin for a discussion. When I entered, I was confronted by a man with his hands at his side who started pushing me around with his chest. There was a third person in the cabin, a signalman who was obviously there to act as a witness. It was a blatant attempt to get me sacked after thirty-five years of service. It failed, but I was thoroughly disgusted with management. I never received any explanation or apology for this incident.

There is a saying: 'He who lives by the sword dies by it.' A few years later, I was told, the manager involved in this incident was at a meeting, he responded angrily to one of the attendees, who was throwing rolled-up paper at him. I have heard the manager's employment was terminated as a result.

I can see the railway system making a revival in years to come, but not in the same form as we have at present. To have an efficient working system, the gauge has to be uniform to alleviate necessary transhipping at state borders. A standard gauge across the board would take ten hours' travel out of the system and be competitive with road transport. It could also lead to the building of track through the middle of Queensland to allow longer and higher trains. These trains could then be filled with drive-on drive-off freight, with pick-up points at various intervals between, and eventually be remote driven. It would also put life back into the west.

Our next lot of grandchildren started to arrive in 2010, when Ryan's first son, Aden, was born, followed by Jennie's third daughter, Sophie, in 2012. After that came Ryan's second son, Jackson, in 2013, followed by Keryn's first son, Lewis. Our other daughter, Angela, was next, giving birth to Hugo, who also has ginger hair.

When we have a gathering now, there are three 'rangers' (ranger is a nickname given to redheaded people; also, Flynn like to be called a 'ranger'). All of our children and our ten grandchildren live within a twenty-minute drive of our home, and have filled up our house with cots, strollers and toys again. As I completed this book, we were presented with our newest granddaughter, Elsie Gweneth, a sister to Lewis.

My father died in 2002, and I made the trip to Maryborough. With help, I cleaned out the garage where he had stashed all his things. I imagine him laughing as we took three loads of old lawnmowers plus another three loads of pushbikes to the Maryborough dump. When we arrived with the first load, we were asked where it all came from. When I said 'Stan Scott' they laughed and said, 'Welcome home, bikes and mowers.' It had all come from the dump originally.

My mum spent her last few years in a nursing home, and enjoyed her time there. Her washing was done for her, and her meals were supplied; for once in her life all she had to do was read the newspaper and watch television. She deserved her time of peace in the nursing home. Mum died peacefully in 2004.

I volunteer drive for the Mater Hospital in Brisbane, conveying patients to and from appointments. This is a most rewarding and satisfying position. The interaction with patients and some of the life stories they tell me are very interesting.

I started to travel overseas a couple of years ago, and every March I travel to Vietnam and work as a volunteer rebuilding kindergartens. Project Vietnam sends a team of thirty plus people to Vietnam and Cambodia, and for a fortnight they work alongside the locals. The end result is a freshly constructed building, and on our last Friday there we conduct a handover ceremony in which we eat and drink with our new workmates. We follow this by presenting every child with a small bag of goodies.

During the appropriate months I take out my little tinny to one of the local creeks and catch mud crabs. I also go to bed early. When I'm asked why, I reply, 'Because I can.'

Jackie and I purchased a motorhome and travelled around the country a few times, then sold it when we realised it was doing nothing but sit in the yard for long periods. I purchased a pop-up caravan, and I now travel with my mate Geoff Nash from Sydney on once-a-year trips.

In 2012 I visited my sister Lorraine in Kingaroy, and while I was there I received a call from the police in Townsville to say that our big brother Robert had passed away. I went to Townsville with another brother, Stuart, who lived in Kingaroy, and after seeing to all the arrangements we laid Robert to rest at the age of sixty-nine.

At a later date, I returned to Townsville with my other brother Neil to finish tidying up Robert's estate, and clean out his unit for sale. This was when I realised that the last time I'd seen Robert was at the boarding house in Brisbane, when he was twenty-seven.

I felt bad about this, and tried to work out the reason behind the lack of contact. I realised that once he had settled in Far North Queensland, Robert never ventured south again and I never went to Townsville. This was not good enough, and the guilt really affected me. I hoped that after Neil and I had renovated the unit I would feel differently. It took three weeks before we were able to put the unit on the market, and I still felt the same guilt.

The unit sold for a fair price, but I still needed closure. I didn't know Neil's feelings on this subject since our discussions never went that deep. Eventually I came to a peaceful resolution that enabled me to move on. My sister Lorraine and I are the same type of family-oriented people, but Robert was always the solitary type and liked his own company. This also applied to my other two brothers. Lorraine and I have spoken at different times about this issue and we both try to keep the door open to the others, but when the communication is only one way, eventually you start giving up.

I went back to Maryborough on one of my trips as acting manager and had a look at the piece of railway track at the old Maryborough Station that I had polished on my first day. Like me, it looked old and rusty.

NOTE FROM THE AUTHOR

In the process of writing this book I became aware of how my confidence had grown as I progressed through the various grades of the railway system. As a sixteen-year-old just starting out, I was a follower. When I came to the end of a deeply satisfying career, I realised I had become a leader.

Please feel free to contact me. My email address is: railwaylifesn041154@gmail.com.

ACKNOWLEDGEMENTS

A very big thanks goes to my wife Jackie and family, and the wives of all my workmates, for their constant support during our working lives, including putting up with our moods after working night shift and not getting enough sleep. It's been a long road but we've made it through to the end.

I was lucky to have worked with great coordinators at Acacia Ridge: Keith Thomas, Richard Shaw, Darryl Richter, and after Darryl retired, Alan Pyke.

Likewise the coordinators at Fisherman Island: Allan Beitz, Allan Mead, John Barker and Ray Lynch, who worked with us in tandem on each shift to ensure we achieved the correct end result.

I thoroughly enjoyed my railway life. Over the years I met some real characters and made some great friends, and always remembered, since the day I first started at Mayne Junction, to keep my workplace a happy and safe one.

I have never suffered fools well; at various times that has been obvious.

Thanks to Book Cover Cafe for assisting me in my maiden journey through the publishing world, from first draft to editing; especially Penny, for her patience and persistence in making sure I wrote the book in the correct sequence with regard to family and feelings.

A very special thanks goes to Yvonne Richardson for spending her valuable time drawing sketches of the various railway items. Jackie and I met Yvonne and David on a cruise and have remained very good friends since.

Big thanks also go to Geoff and Maree Nash who assisted me in the early stages of putting the book to/gether in some form for the editing process by Bookcover Cafe,I will always be greatfull for that help.

Special thanks to Rae and Ken Scott, for allowing me to include their family and working life in my book.

If for some reason I have offended anyone through my wording in the book, please accept my apologies. My intention was not to offend anyone but to record what actually happened during those times.

www.ingramcontent.com/pod-product-compliance
Lightning Source LLC
Chambersburg PA
CBHW052308300426
44110CB00035B/2172